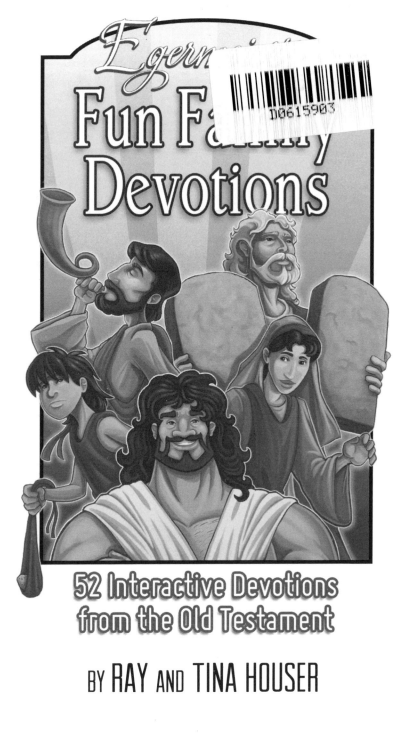

Egermeier's
Fun Family
Devotions

52 Interactive Devotions from the Old Testament

BY RAY AND TINA HOUSER

Warner
Press

Egermeier's® Fun Family Devotions

52 Interactive Lessons from the Old Testament

By Ray and Tina Houser

Scripture references marked (NIV) are taken from *Holy Bible, New International Version*®, NIV® Copyright © 1973, 1978, 1984, 2011 by Biblica, Inc.® Used by permission. All rights reserved worldwide.

Scripture referencs marked (NASB) are taken from the *New American Standard Bible* (NASB). Copyright© 1960,1962,1963,1968,1971,1972,1973,1975,1977,1995 by The Lockman Foundation.

Unmarked scripture references are from the *King James Version*. Public domain.

©2013 by Warner Press Inc Anderson, IN 46018

www.warnerpress.org

ISBN: 978-1-59317-725-6

Editors: Robin Fogle, Karen Rhodes

Design & Illustrations: Curt Corzine & Christian Elden

Printed in USA

Table Of Contents

Introduction

Family devotions… What thoughts and emotions does that term conjure up? Yawns? Eyes rolling? Boring? Regimented? Bible drills? Well, hold on, because we want to help you change that mindset!

Family devotion time is not about having hour-long, perfect, amazing, ground-shaking, deeply spiritual devotions that change the course of lives from that moment on. It's about building a foundation of faith by diving into God's Word together. It's about being purposeful and intentional with your family time.

Elsie Egermeier wrote a phenomenal Bible story book that Bible scholars agree is biblically accurate and in chronological order. The devotional guide you're holding right now is a way to take what Egermeier began and add some family fun time to reinforce the Bible story.

Each of the 52 devotional times consists of three components. The first section is for parents, and provides some in-depth Bible background, how that story connects to Scripture, how it points toward Jesus, and some questions to ponder. The second section is a fun activity to do as a family if you have preschoolers, and the third section is a fun activity to do as a family if you have elementary age kids. The things you'll need to gather for those games and activities should be easy to find around your home.

The family fun activities are not meant for you to hand off to your kids to do by themselves. We want you to do them together. Families have busy schedules, but actually do very little together. When you go to a child's game, you all go, but you're not doing something together. When you're home, everyone is busy with their own thing and you're not really together. This family fun time is intended to be a few minutes when you're all together, doing something that everyone enjoys, and basing it all on a Bible story.

FAMILY
DEVOTIONS
=
FUN!

FOR PARENTS:
STORY BACKGROUND
THINK & TALK

FOR PRESCHOOLERS:
FUN TIMES WITH
YOUNGER KIDS

FOR ELEMENTARY
AGE KIDS:
FUN TIMES WITH
OLDER KIDS

1

The 52 family fun time devotions in this book do not cover all the Old Testament stories in Egermeier's. We recommend you read through *Egermeier's® Bible Story Book*, and when you come to a story connected to one of these devotions, declare a family fun night. You will want to read the complete devotion prior to family time, so you can decide what background information you'd like to share, what questions to ask, and how, when and where to play the game or do the activity.

You've got years to impact your child for Christ. The little moments you take each and every day add up. Let us encourage you to speak truth into and over your child every chance you get.

Deuteronomy 6:6-7 (NASB) says, *These words, which I am commanding you today, shall be on your heart. You shall teach them diligently to your sons and shall talk of them when you sit in your house and when you walk by the way and when you lie down and when you rise up.* Kids are with their children's pastor for an average of one hour each 168-hour week. The other 167 hours they are in the care of their parents. Last time we checked, the children's pastor wasn't there when you got up in the morning or when you sent your kids off to bath time! Being responsible for the spiritual formation of your child is an important task, and it requires being aware of it every single hour of the week.

This book is a tool that will help you grab a few minutes together…playing…laughing…talking…and all around the theme of a Bible story. Enjoy!

 RAY AND TINA HOUSER

How the World Was Made
[GENESIS 1:1–2:24]

Bible Story Time

Read "How the World Was Made" in your *Egermeier's® Bible Story Book*.

Story Background

This story is the basis for our belief in the existence of God, our knowledge of Him, and our faith in His love and care. *In the beginning God created...* (Genesis 1:1) is the starting point for everything. If we believe that God was there in the beginning and made everything in our universe, then the rest of the Bible is the story of His interaction with us, and His desire for a relationship with all people.

The creation story has become controversial for some. Scientists insist that creation took millennia, while strict creationists say it took six days, as we understand a "day." At first glance, the idea of six days seems obvious, but throughout the Bible the term "day" does not necessarily refer to a 24-hour period. The prophets refer to "the Day of the Lord" and the "day of small things." The Apostle Peter wrote, *But do not forget this one thing, dear friends: With the Lord a day is like a thousand years, and a thousand years are like a day* (2 Peter 3:8, NIV). Also, in our everyday language, the word "day" often refers to a period of time as in: "the day of the steam engine" or "the days of yore."

While the creation story may or may not be specific on the timeframe, it is specific about something that is far more important. God created the heavens and earth and everything else. That is the important take away fact for all of us. The first thing we learn about God is that He is the Creator of all we know and can know. Science is man's effort to explain how God did it and how it all works. The explanatory theories change, but the fact that God is responsible doesn't change.

Human beings are the crowning creative achievement of God's creation. We are unique because we are made in His image.

MILLENNIA = 1000 YEARS

Therefore, we have the ability to think about and worship God. No other creature has that ability. We also have the responsibility to take care of the rest of creation. No other creature has that responsibility. The God who created everything gave human beings a special place in that creation.

Think & Talk

How does being the only creature created in the image of God make us different from all the others?

What privileges go along with being created in His image? What responsibilities?

Fun Times with Younger Kids

Say: God created everything in this big, big world! He made it all.

Go outside and spend some time identifying things that God made. Choose a color and find all the things you can with that color on them. Each time someone names something God created, he or she should hit knuckles with someone else's knuckles and then open your hands wide as arms are raised. The hands become a little fireworks' explosion. As the child celebrates God's creation this way, he or she should shout, "God made it! Whooo!"

Fun Times with Older Kids

Needed: camera

Note: You may want to work together on this project for a week. Kids love to take pictures, so make sure your child knows how to handle a camera properly.

MAKE A VIDEO SLIDE SHOW WITH MUSIC FOR A KEEPSAKE FOR YOUR KIDS!

God created everything in six days. Take a photo to represent each day. You may need more than one picture to show what you want to say. Print out the pictures and make a creation scrapbook.

Day 1: Light and darkness
Day 2: Divide the water—water above and water below
Day 3: Dry land, the seas, plants
Day 4: Sun, moon, stars
Day 5: Water creatures, birds of the air
Day 6: Land animals and people

The First Home
[GENESIS 2:8–3:24]

Bible Story Time

Read "The First Home" in your *Egermeier's® Bible Story Book*.

Story Background

The story of Adam and Eve is the story of many of mankind's "firsts."

First temptation. The serpent, an embodiment of Satan, tempted Adam and Eve the same way he still tempts people. He told Eve a half-truth. In effect, he convinced her that if she did a foolish thing—disobeying God—it would result in a good thing—being as wise as God. Then, she and Adam would be able to discern good and evil. Knowing good from evil is only a part of wisdom. Full wisdom consists in refraining from *doing* evil.

First sin. Eve and Adam ate the fruit from the forbidden tree of the knowledge of good and evil. Eating the fruit was the result of the real sin—disobeying God. From that point on, everyone has been born with the sin of disobedience.

First and second "passing of the buck." When God asked Adam if he had eaten the forbidden fruit, Adam told God that Eve gave it to him. Then Eve said it was the serpent's fault. There's lots of finger-pointing going on here.

First punishment. Adam and Eve could no longer walk with God in the Garden, but now would have to scratch out a living. God told them it would be hard. Perhaps, we should think about that when we wonder why our lives are difficult. Since God guaranteed that life outside the Garden would be difficult, we should be thankful and feel especially blessed when times are easy.

This story sets the stage for the rest of the Bible. Obviously, we see the beginning of the battle between good and evil, and

BEING #1 ISN'T ALWAYS BEST.

5

between holiness and sin. Yet we also see God's pursuit of people. God said, "Adam, where are you?" The rest of the Bible is the story of God seeking a relationship with us.

Think & Talk

What half-truths does Satan use today to tempt people? To tempt you?

When have you been blessed beyond your right to expect blessings?

In what ways does God pursue a relationship with people today?

Fun Times with Younger Kids

Needed: piece of cardboard, ping-pong balls

Tear a piece, like one of the flaps, off a cardboard box for each person. Set some ping-pong balls together in the middle of the floor.

Say: These ping-pong balls will be Adam and Eve. This room is the Garden. When the ping-pong balls go through the doorway and into the next room, they're like Adam and Eve leaving the Garden.

At the signal, everyone will wave their piece of cardboard close to the balls. The moving air caused from the flapping cardboard should make the ping-pong balls move. Keep waving the cardboard until you're able to get all of the ping-pong balls through a doorway and out of the room.

Say: "Sin" is when we do or say something that God doesn't want us to do or say. Sin is when we disobey God. When Adam and Eve sinned—disobeyed God—God made Adam and Eve leave the Garden. He wouldn't allow them to stay there. They had to live outside the Garden now. When they were in the Garden, they just got to enjoy everything and there were no problems. Even when they left the Garden, God still took care of Adam and Eve, but they had to work hard.

SIN SEPARATES US FROM GOD.

Needed: dominoes, masking tape

Find as many dominoes as you can—the more you have, the more fun it will be. Place some 1" pieces of masking tape on a hard floor to indicate a flowing path.

Note: To make curved lines with masking tape is difficult, so just keep in mind that you are making a curved line by going from one piece of masking tape to the next. You want this line to be gradual and not have harsh turns.

Now, have everyone work together to set dominoes on end along the path. Position them about an inch from one another. After you have all the dominoes set up, choose one person to gently tap the end domino.

Say: What happened? The action of one domino falling caused the next domino to fall, and so on and so on. How does this remind you of what happened when Adam and Eve sinned? Each time you and I disobey God, it affects someone else. When they see that you think it's okay to disobey God, then they may think it's okay for them to disobey Him also. How does lying act like dominoes? How can gossip be like dominoes? Name some more ways that your sin affects someone else.

ONE SIN CAN HAVE A NEGATIVE EFFECT ON MANY PEOPLE.

The Great Flood
[GENESIS 5:1–9:17]

Bible Story Time

Read "The Great Flood" in your *Egermeier's® Bible Story Book.*

Story Background

THE ARK'S TOTAL DECK AREA WAS EQUIVALENT TO THE AREA OF ABOUT 20 STANDARD COLLEGE BASKETBALL COURTS

The early literature of nearly all ancient cultures includes a great flood story. Obviously, this flood took place before writing was invented so we don't have a date, but the fact that this story in some form is nearly universal is evidence that the flood really happened. The story's message is that man strayed so far from God, He decided to start over. Apparently, God was down to one friend in the world—Noah—so Noah became the person God chose to continue what He began with Adam and Eve.

Basically, Noah did what Adam and Eve did not do—he obeyed God. God told Noah to build a boat, a HUGE boat, far from any body of water. Noah trusted God. When his neighbors told him to wise up and quit working on the ark, it must have been hard to keep working, but Noah continued to trust.

The plans for the ark are interesting. In this huge boat, there is only one door. Think about that. There was only one way to get to safety, to be rescued from the flood—from death. God's Word makes it very clear that there is only one way for us to be saved from our disobedience—our sin—against God and that is through believing in Jesus Christ. Jesus is even referred to as the Door in John 10:7. Friends, family, and the media may try to convince you that there are many ways to get to heaven, like through good deeds or believing in just about anything as long as you're sincere about whatever it is you believe. The truth is that everyone can be included…everyone can have a relationship with God…no matter the culture, race, sex, socio-economic condition, *but there is only one way, one Door—Jesus.*

Noah and the ark gave the world a second chance. When we trust in Christ, repent of our sins and live in love and obedience to the Lord, we have a second chance. Our lives become as fresh and new as the world after the flood. He stands ready to join us in an eternal relationship when we end our rebellion and trust Him.

Think & Talk

When have you ignored God's voice like the people who did not enter the ark?

Share with your children your personal experience of accepting the one Door—Jesus Christ. How did that change your life? Your kids need to hear this over and over, as part of their family story.

Fun Times with Younger Kids

Sing "Old MacDonald Had a Farm" together, only change the wording to:

God told Noah to build an ark … e-i-e-i-o.

And on that ark he put a _____ … e-i-e-i-o.

Expand your animals to include jungle, desert, forest, as well as farm animals. This is a good time to introduce some new animals to your child. Get out some animal picture books to cue you during the song. Why not make this the new way you *always* sing this song!

Fun Times with Older Kids

Needed: 6 containers, socks

Say: The ark had only one door that led Noah and his family, along with all the animals, safely back to dry land after the storm. If they didn't go through that door, then they wouldn't be saved. The Bible tells us that there is only one Door that will lead us back to God, and that Door is Jesus Christ. Other people will try to convince you that it doesn't matter what you believe, just that you believe in something. God welcomes everyone, but He has given us only one way to be saved from the consequences of our disobedience.

You'll need several pair of socks and 6 large containers (buckets, tubs, large cooking pots). Set them close together on

A TRIP TO THE ZOO IS A FUN WAY TO SEE UNUSUAL ANIMALS!

9

the floor and mark only one as the right one. Roll each pair of socks into itself to make a soft ball. Each person will take a turn tossing the socks at the one correct pot. Each time a sock ball goes in the marked container, the person must say, "There's only one way to God!" You can give each other a crazy amount of points for each successful toss and no score for hitting the other containers.

Abram Follows God
[GENESIS 11:27–12:20]

Bible Story Time *Egermeier's*

Read "Abram Follows God" in your *Egermeier's®* Bible Story Book.

Story Background

Abram's family were nomads, shepherds who lived wherever they could find grass and water for their sheep. They started out in an ancient city called Ur, on the Euphrates River. That place is now in the country known as Iraq. This land was considered the center of civilization, but Abram's family were not city people. They moved up the Euphrates to Haran, and finally Abram followed the call of God to leave that comparatively rich land to go to Canaan, known today as Israel.

The interesting part of this story is that Abram left the familiar lands to go to Canaan because he heard God calling him to go. He wasn't even sure where he was going. God only said that He would show him. What an incredible faith Abram had! He moved his wife, nephew Lot, their servants, livestock and tents to a land completely unknown to them. They had to walk by faith because that was all they had to go on. Abram moved until he got the word from God that he was where God wanted him to be.

God promised to bless the world through Abram and his family. As it turned out, Abram's family would later be known as the Jews and from them—many, many years later—God's Son, Jesus, would be born. Of course, Abram didn't know all that then. He just knew that God called him to go to a place that would be shown to him. God alone could see the outcome of Abram's obedience and faith.

In the same way you cannot know the consequences of following the Lord. As you build a strong, faithful family, you can't know what great things will come of it, anymore than

UR WAS LOCATED
BETWEEN
BAGHDAD, IRAQ,
AND THE TIP
OF THE
PERSIAN GULF
IN THE
MIDDLE EAST.

Abram did. Who knows how your faithfulness now will affect your family's future or even the future of the world! Here's your assurance—God knows.

Think & Talk

When has God challenged you to do something out of the ordinary? How did you respond? Is He challenging you now? If so, how?

How do you think your being faithful to the Lord will affect your children?

Ask God to help you see a glimpse of His perspective of your life.

Fun with Younger Kids

Needed: sheets, blankets, flashlights, snack

Round up an assortment of sheets and blankets that can be draped over chairs and tables. Create a tent large enough that the entire family can get under it. Pull out a flashlight and read the story of Abram while in your tent.

MAKE MEMORIES BY TAKING THIS ACTIVITY OUTSIDE WITH A REAL TENT & CAMPFIRE.

Say: Can you imagine living in a tent? Because Abram lived in a tent, he could move around fairly easily. It's fun for us to play in a tent every once in a while, but living in one all the time would get old.

Share a snack together inside the tent and sing a song or two. Be prepared; your kids will want to keep the tent up for a day or two because it's just so much fun!

Fun Times with Older Kids

Needed: 4 paper plates, 6 milk caps, 2 long sticks

For the 2 long sticks, you can use broom handles, yardsticks, dowel rods, or golf clubs (play or real). Designate 3 points, such as a chair in the middle of the room, a floor lamp in the corner, and a book bag by the door.

Say: Abram moved from place to place. Each time God instructed him to go to a new place, Abram packed up all his belongings and family, then herded his sheep and other livestock to their new home.

Two people will play at a time. Each person will put a paper plate under each foot and place 3 milk caps in front of them. The milk caps represent the livestock that have to be herded. At the signal, both players will move their 3 milk caps to the first designated point (chair in the middle of the room), then to the second point (floor lamp), and then to the third point (book bag) by using only their stick and while keeping both feet on their paper plates.

Say: How do you think it would feel to move all the time and have a temporary tent home? Why did Abram willingly pick up and move? What can you learn about yourself from Abram?

PAPER PLATE WALKING IS NOT AS EASY AS IT SOUNDS!

Hagar and Ishmael
[GENESIS 20:1–21:21]

Egermeier's **Bible Story Time**

Read "Hagar and Ishmael" in your *Egermeier's®* Bible Story Book.

Story Background

TO FIND OUT
WHY GOD
CHANGED
ABRAM'S AND
SARAI'S NAMES,
READ

GENESIS 17:1-22.

Abram (by this point known as Abraham) must have had a tough time figuring out what the Lord was doing with his life. God had called him to live as a stranger in Canaan and promised to make a great nation of his descendants. The years went by and Abraham and his wife Sarai (now known as Sarah) were getting old. They believed God's promise, but they thought Sarah's time to have a baby had come and gone. Perhaps to help God along with the plan, Abraham fathered a son with Sarah's servant, Hagar. Ishmael was a fine strong boy, but he wasn't what God had in mind. God's intention was that Sarah would bear Abraham a son. And so she did, at a very advanced age. They named him Isaac, which means laughter, because Sarah had laughed at the notion that she would become a mother in her nineties.

Eventually, there was a dispute between the two boys. Sarah did not want Isaac to grow up alongside Ishmael. Abraham was directed by God to send Hagar and Ishmael away, and promised that Ishmael too would father a great nation. God provided for Hagar and Ishmael as they lived and flourished in the desert. Today, the Arabs trace their ancestry to Ishmael, and of course, Israel traces their ancestry to Isaac. It's interesting to note that the current Arab-Israeli controversy has long roots, going all the way back to Genesis.

Abraham and Sarah loved Isaac and brought him up to love and trust God. They taught him well because they believed God would keep His word to begin a nation through Isaac that would bless the world.

Think & Talk

What resulted when Abraham and Sarah tried to help God keep His promise by adding Hagar to the equation?

God gave Isaac to Abraham and Sarah long after they thought parenthood was possible. What was God teaching them by waiting so long to meet their needs?

What has God taught you in a time of waiting?

Fun Times with Younger Kids

Needed: empty water bottles, soup kettle

Fill one side of your kitchen sink with water. Place the soup kettle in the other sink. Show your child how to push an empty water bottle under the water, squeeze the bottle, then release it so water fills the bottle. Once the bottle is full, pour it into the kettle. Keep doing this until the kettle is full. If it's a pretty day, take this outside and run it like a relay.

Say: Hagar and her son, Ishmael, were out in the desert, and they were very thirsty. God provided some water that bubbled up out of the ground for them. Hagar filled her empty bottle with the water and gave it to Ishmael.

HAGAR AND ISHMAEL WERE LOST IN THE DESERT OF BEERSHEBA.

Fun Times with Older Kids

Needed: balloon, rope/masking tape

Say: God told Abraham and Sarah they would have a son. God didn't say Hagar would be the mother; the mother would be Sarah. But, Abraham and Sarah stepped out of bounds and took things into their own hands. Why did they do this? Were they impatient with God?

This game can be set up inside or outside. Using rope or masking tape, mark two parallel lines about 8 feet apart. Two people will play at a time. Each player will stand in front of one of the lines, facing each other. Inflate a balloon and bat it back and forth. The object is to keep the balloon from going out of bounds—past your line. Each time it does go out, the two players must yell, "Out of bounds!"

Abraham Offers Isaac
[GENESIS 22:1–19]

Egermeier's **Bible Story Time**

Read "Abraham Offers Isaac" in your *Egermeier's® Bible Story Book*.

Story Background

God's instructions must have been devastating. Abraham had grown to love and treasure his son Isaac. Then, suddenly, God told Abraham to offer the boy on an altar of sacrifice—to give the boy back to God by killing him. The heartbreak and confusion that must have flooded Abraham's soul are hard to imagine. God had given him this son and promised great things for him and the family, but now the boy was to be killed.

Child sacrifice was far from unknown in the ancient world. Worshippers of the god Molech in Canaan would throw children through the mouth of their idol into a fire. It was horrible, and it was the last thing Abraham thought God would demand of him.

THE BIBLE REFERS TO JESUS AS THE LAMB. READ ISAIAH 53:7 & JOHN 1:29.

By age twelve, Isaac had probably accompanied Abraham many times to worship God and sacrifice lambs or cattle. This time was different because they went a long way to a special mountain. (This mountain is thought to be the same place where Solomon would build the temple for God many centuries later.) As Abraham and Isaac drew close to the site for the sacrifice, Isaac realized they had brought no animal and asked where the lamb was. Abraham simply said, "God will provide the lamb." He knew God had provided Isaac to him as a son and now, if Isaac was the sacrifice he must give, he would do it. Of course, we know God stopped the sacrifice and provided a ram, caught in a thicket. The Bible says the ram was caught by the horns, and that is an important thing to notice. Since it was caught by the horns, the ram had no blemish. It would not have cuts from the briars on the bush. This sacrifice—and the sacrifice of the perfect Lamb of God—was without blemish.

Three things resulted from this unfinished sacrifice. 1) God's people knew for certain that child sacrifice was not what their God required. 2) Though this terrible sacrifice was not required in the end, God is, in fact, first priority. We must be obedient to do whatever He asks of us. 3) And, the stage is set for God to provide the Lamb for the ultimate sacrifice—the God/man Jesus—on the cross for the sins of us all.

Think & Talk

God doesn't want us to sacrifice our children to Him, but how can we properly treat them as God's gift lent to us to raise?

To what things have you seen modern parents sacrifice their children? (Ex. career, hobby, personal pleasure)

What correlations do you make between Abraham offering Isaac and God offering His Son?

Fun Times with Younger Kids

Each person will retrieve 3 things that are their most important possessions. If the object can't be picked up easily (like a car), then choose something to represent it (like a set of keys). These are THINGS, not people. Give each person a chance to tell why these things are important.

Say: Let's suppose that God asked you to give Him one of your favorite things. Which is your most favorite? Would you be willing to give it away if God asked you to? God is not asking you to give away your favorite things, but He wants to know that He is more important than anything you have.

GOD IS MORE IMPORTANT THAN THINGS!

Fun Times with Older Kids

Needed: Bibles, 3 plastic disposable plates, 3 empty pop cans

Say: God promised Abraham that he would be the father of a great nation. Abraham trusted God to keep that promise. Even though the promise seemed impossible, Abraham's trust in God was greater than his doubt. God rewarded Abraham for trusting that He knew better and would keep His promise.

Below are some verses that mention a promise of God. Look up one verse and tell what God promised. Your reward for identifying the promise is to tackle the plate/can challenge. It may seem impossible, but it's not!

Float a plastic disposable plate in a full sink of water. Set an empty can in the center of the plate. Set another plate on top of the can. Then, set another empty can on the plate, aligned with the can underneath. The challenge is to get three plates and three cans on top of one another, floating in the sink. You only have 90 seconds to get it done, though! When you accomplish your challenge (or run out of time), look up another promise and have a second try at the challenge.

Genesis 18:14
Deuteronomy 4:29
Joshua 1:9
Psalm 55:22
Proverbs 1:7
Acts 17:27-28
Romans 8:28
Philippians 1:6

Esau Sells His Birthright
[GENESIS 25:19-34]

Bible Story Time *Egermeier's*

Read "Esau Sells His Birthright" in your *Egermeier's*® *Bible Story Book.*

Story Background

Abraham's son Isaac had two sons. In the days of Isaac and his sons, Esau and Jacob, custom dictated that the first-born son was the main heir. At the death of the father, the first-born got two-thirds of the estate, and the rest of the sons divided the other third. Daughters received nothing. Esau and Jacob were twins. Esau was born first, but Jacob came out with his hand on Esau's heel. Jacob's name means "heel grabber" or "supplanter," one who would take the place of another. As they grew up, Jacob lived up to that name. In this story, he persuades Esau to give up his birthright, and later Jacob steals Isaac's special blessing from Esau as well. Jacob may have been a planner and plotter, but at the same time Esau was careless with something precious.

This story speaks loudly to our world today. Esau gave up his birthright to two-thirds of his father's estate for a bowl of soup. It's all about immediate gratification. He was hungry after a hard day's work, and Jacob's soup smelled so good that Esau convinced himself he couldn't wait, even a little while, for supper.

Over and over again, we see people selling their future for immediate gratification. Credit cards are run up to the limit for clothes that wear out or go out of style before they are paid for. Money is borrowed to have "what I have always wanted"— even if "always" is, in reality, a few days. Later, Esau realized his foolishness and regretted it. Many people today regret for years, and even through eternity, foolish choices they have made. When you hear yourself saying, "I just have to have it," it would be wise to think of Esau and decide if the need for your

"GOOD THINGS COME TO THOSE WHO WAIT." READ ISAIAH 40:31 IN YOUR BIBLE.

object of desire is really worth the long-term cost. This is a very important principle to teach your children, but how can you teach it if you don't live it?

Think & Talk

How are you teaching your children about delayed gratification?

Are you teaching them by your example?

How often do you make your children wait for their heart's desire?

Fun Times with Younger Kids

Needed: ingredients for soup, can opener, soup kettle, tortilla chips

This is a great recipe for preschoolers to help with because it consists of opening six cans and pouring them together. The six cans are:

1 15-ounce can of kernel corn, drained
1 10-ounce can chunk chicken
1 15-ounce can black beans
1 10-ounce can diced tomatoes with green chile peppers
2 14-ounce cans chicken broth

Open the cans for your child and let them pour the contents into a big soup kettle. Heat on medium.

Let the soup warm for a while so the smell fills the house. Take the kids outside to breathe fresh air and then re-enter the house. As you come in the house, instruct everyone to take a deep breath.

Say: What do you smell? How does it make your belly feel when you smell something good cooking? The smell makes us even hungrier than we were. I think Esau got really hungry when he smelled the yummy soup that Jacob was cooking, and all he could think about was a delicious meal that he could have.

TRY OTHER FRAGRANT RECIPES LIKE FRESH BAKED BREAD, APPLE PIE OR HOMEMADE SPAGHETTI SAUCE.

Needed: miscellaneous objects

Say: What was Esau's problem? He was hungry. But, his other problem was that he didn't have self-control. He didn't want to wait until he could make himself something to eat. Instead, he traded something very valuable—his birthright—for a bowl of soup! That's a high price to pay for lacking self-control. Having self-control is when you are able to wait, instead of doing something right now. When have you gotten in trouble because you couldn't wait? When have you not had self-control?

For this game, there will be a caller. Everyone else will line up against a wall. Set an object about 4-feet in front of each player. When the caller says, "Ready, Set, Go", then the first person to grab their object gets 100 points. But, the caller may also say, "Ready, Set, ..." and use a different word that begins with the letter "G". So, it could be "Ready, Set, Good" or "Ready, Set, Gopher." Anyone touching their object when the wrong "G" word is said will lose 200 points.

Say: You didn't have self-control, and it cost you lots of points. You couldn't wait for the right "G" word to be said. You reacted without thinking clearly. When we don't have self-control, we can have all kinds of problems. Let's ask God to help us develop strong self-control.

TALK ABOUT A TIME WHEN YOU WAITED AND SOMETHING GREAT HAPPENED.

Jacob and Esau Meet Again
[GENESIS 32–35]

Egermeier's Bible Story Time

Read "Jacob and Esau Meet Again" in your *Egermeier's® Bible Story Book*.

Story Background

Revenge…. Terrible things done in the name of revenge have torn families, friends, and even nations apart. We can easily understand why Esau would want to seek revenge on his scheming brother, Jacob. In fact, Esau had pledged to get revenge on his twin brother after Jacob had tricked him out of his birthright and stolen their father's blessing.

Twenty years passed before Jacob returned to Canaan. Jacob had lived with the fear of facing Esau the entire time he was in Haran. The night before the fateful meeting, Jacob wrestled with an angel of God who changed his name from Jacob, meaning the "supplanter," to Israel, which means "a prince of God." Even though Jacob had this experience with the angel and had his name changed by God, his knees still must have shook the next morning when Esau approached with his 400 men.

To Jacob/Israel's surprise and relief, Esau greeted him not with a sword, but with a brotherly hug. Jacob was sure that Esau had spent 20 years thinking about getting back at him for his treachery. On the contrary, instead of stewing in his anger and planning revenge on Jacob, Esau had built a life. He had a great family and all the wealth he needed. Esau's revenge was not found in hurting Jacob; instead, it was found in going his own way and enjoying the life he had.

How many terrible conflicts and years of hatred could be avoided if more people could manage to do what Esau did? When we hold on to the wrongs others have done to us, we give them a place of undue importance in our lives. The time we spend thinking ill of them and wishing revenge on them is

THE TRIP FROM HARAN TO CANAAN WAS OVER 400 MILES, NOT COUNTING THE DISTANCE OVER MOUNTAINS.

time we could spend building our own lives. As someone once said, "The best revenge is to live well."

Think & Talk

LET'S LEARN TO FORGIVE.

How has someone wronged you?

Have you let go of it?

Why not ask God to enable you to put that person and the circumstance behind you. Ask Him to give you enthusiasm for the life you have before you.

Fun Times with Younger Kids

Needed: magnets, paper clips

Place a paper clip on the table and then move a magnet closer and closer to it, until the paper clip comes to the magnet.

Say: The magnet and the paper clip were separate, but when we moved them closer to each other, they joined together. Let's say the magnet stands for Esau, and the paper clip is Jacob. They had been far apart, but when they both began moving toward one another, they finally joined back together.

Encourage the kids to play with the paper clips and magnets to see how close they have to be before the paper clip will jump toward the magnet. If you have different strength magnets, bring them all out and do some experimenting with their power.

Fun Times with Older Kids

Needed: plain paper, markers, tape

Each person will draw a picture of someone they have had a conflict with. This could be a friend, family member, co-worker, neighbor, or someone at church.

Say: Conflict tears us apart. Jacob and Esau had a terrible conflict that made Jacob fear for his life. He even ran away because he was so afraid of what Esau might do. The conflict separated them for 20 years!

Tear your pictures into 5 or 6 pieces. Think of things you could say or do that would help mend the relationship. Each time someone shares, they will tape 2 pieces together, and then continue to add one more piece at a time until the picture is complete once again.

Say: We don't have to stay in conflict, waiting for the other person to solve the problem. We can do something to help make it better.

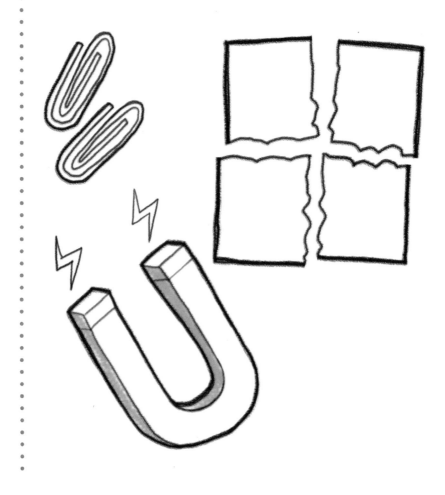

Joseph Becomes a Slave
[GENESIS 37]

Read "Joseph Becomes a Slave" in your *Egermeier's*® Bible Story Book.

Story Background

The moral of the story: Don't mess with your older brothers when Daddy isn't around! That is one lesson we can draw from this story, but that only scratches the surface.

Joseph was Jacob's eleventh son and the first with his favorite wife, Rachel. Perhaps because he was Rachel's boy, or maybe because he was exceptional in other ways, or both, Joseph was Jacob's favorite. Jacob made no secret about it, and his ten older sons grew angry because of it. Joseph, as the object of their anger, only made the situation worse. He was a tattletale, and he may have been a know-it-all. We know for sure that he was a dreamer who used poor judgment when sharing those dreams with others. Big brothers everywhere might say that Joseph was asking for it...and maybe Jacob was too.

A MORAL IS A MESSAGE CONVEYED OR A LESSON TO BE LEARNED FROM A STORY OR EVENT.

The horrible act of the brothers—selling Joseph into slavery—seemed to put an end to their problem, except that their deception sent their father into a tailspin. He still loved Joseph best, even though he thought Joseph was dead.

Many parents have a favorite child: the funny one, the athletic one, the pretty one, the underdog one, the one who is most like them. Yet smart parents work hard to keep that favoritism to themselves and look hard for things to admire in all of their children.

Think & Talk

How are you guarding against favoritism?

How can parents help each other watch for signs of favoritism?

25

Celebrate things each child excels in. Try not to make your children feel they should all be good at the same things, or should all be good at the same thing you excel in.

Fun Times with Younger Kids

Needed: ball

Say: Jacob had lots of children, but one son was his favorite. Do you know what "favorite" means? It's when you like one thing, or person, better than any others. Who was Jacob's favorite son? Joseph. What did Jacob give Joseph that he didn't give to any of his other sons? How do you think that made the brothers feel?

You'll need a ball that is the appropriate size for your child to catch. The entire family will spread out in a large room or outside. Ask the question: "What is your favorite _____?" Toss the ball to a family member who will answer with his or her favorite. Then, that person will toss the ball to the next family member. The last toss should be back to the original tosser, who will then give the next area to name a favorite. (Areas: color, TV show, Bible story, fast food, ice cream, animal, fruit, vegetable, friend, drink, song, room in the house)

Fun Times with Older Kids

Needed: 2 pillowcases, heavy objects

Get out two pillowcases. Leave one empty, but the other one you will put objects in.

Say: Who was jealous in this story? The brothers were jealous of Joseph. Why? When have you been jealous of someone?

Different family members will tell when they have experienced jealousy. Each time a family member shares, they should choose a somewhat heavy object (but not breakable) to put in the pillowcase. These can be objects like: a skillet, a book, a big shoe.

Once the pillowcase is full, do this little exercise. Decide on a course through the house, and then each person will run it two times. The first time, they will run carrying the empty pillowcase. The second time, they will run carrying the full pillowcase.

DON'T LET
JEALOUSY
KEEP YOU
FROM BEING
A WINNER!

Say: Which way was easier to run? Which pillowcase held you back? How is this loaded pillowcase like jealousy? How can jealousy hold you back and slow you down from doing what God has planned for you?

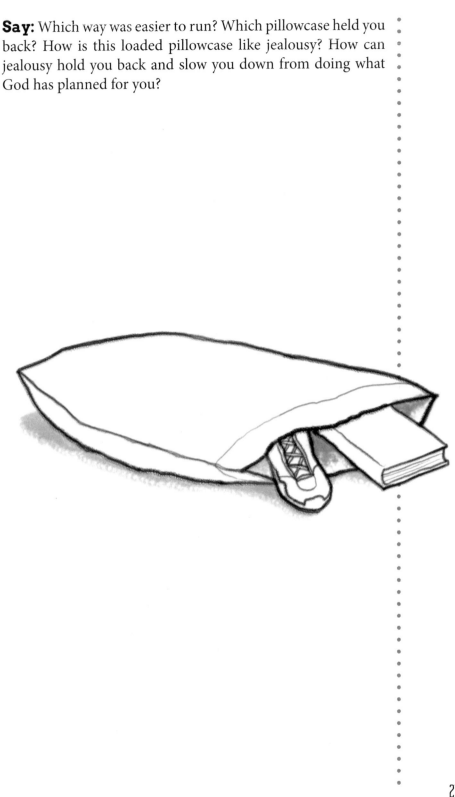

Joseph, a Prisoner in Egypt
[GENESIS 37:36–40:23]

Egermeier's **Bible Story Time**

Read "Joseph, a Prisoner in Egypt" in your *Egermeier's® Bible Story Book*.

Story Background

POTIPHAR WAS CAPTAIN OF THE PALACE GUARD.

For Joseph bad times got worse, and then they got worse again. No one had a better reason to become bitter and cantankerous, but he didn't. He could easily have become sullen and even mean, but he didn't. Instead, Joseph chose to make the best of his situation, whatever it was. Only a slave in Potiphar's house, he soon became the slave-in-charge. Unfairly condemned to prison, he soon became the prisoner-in-charge. He never quit dreaming or interpreting the dreams of others. This young man took whatever life threw at him and remained true to himself and to God. He remained determined not to be ruined by his circumstances. His circumstances changed his life and his prospects, but he wouldn't let them ruin his life.

Some folks are never able to do what Joseph did. A bad break comes their way, and they never get past it. The bad thing becomes the reason for every failure and the excuse for never trying again. Ill health, a bad boss, a failed relationship, an abusive parent or spouse, the death of a loved one, or an economic downturn—all have caused people to retreat from life. When that happens, no one wins except our enemy, Satan. One of these bad circumstances may make your original plans and dreams impossible, but it can't keep you from having a new dream and making new plans, unless you let it. God always has a dream for each of us. Who knows? The second plan might fit us better than the first one anyway.

Think & Talk

When have you let a circumstance or something from your past hold you back?

What circumstances have made you afraid to dream?

Is your life in danger of being ruined by a change in your circumstances?

Ask God for the courage to let Him help you deal with the change. Ask God for a new dream and a new plan.

Fun Times with Younger Kids

Needed: lemons, sugar, strainer, water, pitcher, long-handled spoon

Say: Every time Joseph had something bad happen to him, he relied on God and made it into something better. He had lots of "sour" bad things happen to him too!

If your kids aren't familiar with the taste of raw lemons, let them experience it. Pretty sour! Cut five lemons in half. Show the kids how to squeeze the juice through a strainer to catch the seeds. Put the juice in a pitcher and add 1 c. of sugar. Add 1 cup of hot water and stir until the sugar dissolves. Then, add 2 more cups of really cold water and stir. Enjoy tasting the lemonade you made from sour lemons!

Say: We took something sour and made it into something delicious. This lemonade is a lot better than the sour lemons!

"WHEN LIFE HANDS YOU LEMONS, MAKE LEMONADE!"

Fun Times with Older Kids

Needed: 8 half-sheets of paper, fan

Lay the 8 half-sheets of paper on the floor in front of the fan. Take turns letting one person at a time try to control the papers when the fan is turned on. You cannot pick them up with your hands, but can pin them against something or step on them.

Say: What would make this easier? If you had someone to help you, right? How did it feel to try to accomplish this without help? How is this like our relationship with God? When all these things happened to Joseph, he could've felt like his life was out of control. But Joseph relied on God. When do things feel out of control for you? How can you rely more on God in those times?

Joseph, a Ruler in Egypt
[GENESIS 41]

Egermeier's Bible Story Time

Read "Joseph, a Ruler in Egypt" in your *Egermeier's® Bible Story Book*.

Story Background

One thing that sets Joseph apart from most people is that he was ready when his opportunity came. He made the best of bad situations by continuing to look for his chance to get out of prison and make an impact. Maybe his greatest hope was to return to his father's tent, but while God didn't give him that wish, He did provide Joseph with a one-of-a-kind opportunity. Joseph had always been a dreamer and an interpreter of dreams. Because he interpreted two of his own dreams to his family, he wound up a slave. He interpreted the dreams of two of his fellow prison inmates and received no thanks. Finally, when Pharaoh was troubled by a perplexing dream, one of those old inmates who happened to be a servant of Pharaoh, remembered Joseph's dream-reading ability. Joseph not only interpreted Pharaoh's dream, but also came up with a plan to save Egypt from the coming famine, which the dream predicted.

ALL OF THE KINGS OF EGYPT ARE CALLED PHARAOH.

Pharaoh liked Joseph and the plan so well he made him a kind of prime minister, in charge of implementing the plan. The plan worked, and Joseph became Pharaoh's right-hand man. At last the boy who dreamed of being in charge *was* in charge. More importantly, he was in charge of not only his father's family but the greatest empire of the day!

Think & Talk

How have you developed your talents and readied yourself for the day a great opportunity comes your way? Or have you given up on that degree? That job? That dream?

Are you watching for your chance? Joseph's opportunity was not the one he was looking for, but it was a great one.

Are you open to something that may be new or different for you?

Fun Times with Younger Kids

Make an obstacle course out of chairs, pillows, and other objects in your house. If it's nice weather, take this activity outside. Be very clear what your preschooler needs to do, where to go around, when to hop over, and so on. This is very good for their order development as well as their coordination.

Say: Joseph had some things that got in his way, like being a prisoner, being accused of doing something he didn't do, and being forgotten by the cupbearer when he told him what his dream meant. Joseph kept relying on God and following God's directions. That's how he was able to get around his obstacles. You got around your obstacles by listening to my directions when we started.

Fun Times with Older Kids

Play a video game with your child—one that has obstacles to get around. Yep, you heard me right…play a video game!

Say: We had lots of obstacles to get around in this game. What kind of obstacles did Joseph have? What was waiting on the other side of the obstacles in our game? How was Joseph rewarded by Pharaoh? God had a plan for Joseph, but he had to endure and be faithful to find out what it was.

TRUST GOD AND DON'T LET THE OBSTACLES STOP YOU!

Joseph's Family Moves to Egypt
[GENESIS 45:25–50:26]

Egermeier's Bible Story Time

Read "Joseph's Family Moves to Egypt" in your *Egermeier's® Bible Story Book*.

Story Background

IN BIBLE TIMES PEOPLE SURVIVED ON WHAT THEY COULD GROW THEMSELVES. SEVEN YEARS OF FAMINE WOULD HAVE LIKELY ENDED THE EGYPTIAN NATION.

Joseph led the Egyptians to prepare for a great famine, and when it struck they were able not only to feed themselves but also to sell grain to people from other countries. Among those who came to the Egyptians were Joseph's brothers. Although Joseph recognized them, he didn't reveal himself to them right away. He hoped they had changed somehow in the 20 years since they had sold him into slavery. After watching and testing them, he finally introduced himself to them and asked about their father, Jacob. At his invitation the brothers brought Jacob and all their family to live in Egypt, where everyone including Pharaoh treated them very well.

The plot thickened, however, after Jacob died. The brothers feared that Joseph had been nice to them for the sake of their old father. They feared that with Jacob dead, Joseph would seek revenge for the cruel and ruthless way they had treated him. They went so far as to offer to become his slaves. At that moment Joseph showed how big his heart was. He refused their offer, saying it was not his place to punish them, but God's. He told them, *You intended to harm me, but God intended it for good to accomplish what is now being done, the saving of many lives* (Genesis 50:20, NIV). Joseph was able to see that God had turned his brothers' evil act into something good.

Think & Talk

When have you seen a bad event in your life turned into something good?

Name a setback in your life.

How could a setback you might now be experiencing be turned

to your advantage and the advantage of others? If that is to happen, you will need to get past the desire for revenge and let God have your entire situation.

Ask God to give you the faith and trust you need. Ask Him to turn the bad into something that is good for you and/or someone you love.

Fun Times with Younger Kids

Needed: piece of clothing with buttons (sweater, shirt, jacket)

This is an object lesson, so go slowly. When you begin, have the piece of clothing completely buttoned up. Unbutton as you talk.

Say: People go their separate ways like Joseph's family did. They get angry or jealous of one another, and families can have fights. They come apart like this sweater came apart when I unbuttoned it. We don't want to be angry or jealous of one another, do we? When we reach out, forgive, and welcome others, we can come back together. That's what Joseph did for his brothers.

Encourage your child to button the item of clothing. With each button, say "forgive", "reach out" and "welcome," and ask them to repeat the words after you. This is a great exercise for preschoolers.

Fun Times with Older Kids

Say: Joseph and his family were separated by hard feelings and by many miles. I bet there were many times when Joseph wished he could talk with his father and brothers, but at that time there were no phones or computers. I also think that there were times when his brothers wondered what had happened to Joseph and wished they could hear his voice.

HOW DID PEOPLE COMMUNICATE 100 YEARS AGO?

1000 YEARS AGO?

Do you have someone in your family who lives far away? This is the perfect time to connect with them through Skype, e-mail, or texting a picture. If you have a photo of a family reunion or big holiday dinner, look at it and decide whose voice you would like to hear. Then as a family figure out a way that you could connect across the miles.

A Baby and a Basket
(EXODUS 1:1–2:10)

Egermeier's **Bible Story Time**

Read "A Baby in a Basket" in your *Egermeier's® Bible Story Book.*

Story Background

Four hundred years had passed since the time of Joseph. His family, now called the Israelites, had grown into a large minority group in Egypt. The Pharaoh now on the throne had no reason to favor the Israelites. In fact, he was afraid they were becoming too numerous to control. He made their living conditions difficult and made a cruel decree designed to drive down their population. Every male baby was to be thrown into the Nile River. Into this terrible situation, Moses was born.

LOCATED IN NORTHEASTERN AFRICA, THE NILE RIVER IS THE LONGEST RIVER IN THE WORLD.

Apparently, Moses' mother couldn't bear to watch her baby boy drown, so she made a waterproof basket, put him in it, and set him afloat. Perhaps she knew where the princess of Egypt swam and placed the basket in that area in the vain hope that her boy might be rescued. That hope was answered, and God provided a greater blessing. Moses' sister, Miriam, saw the princess discover the basket and quickly told her that she knew a lady who would be glad to take care of the boy for her.

So Moses remained in his mother's arms, at least until he was weaned. Then he was raised as a prince of Egypt and received a royal education. God had a plan for this baby. The princess named him Moses, meaning "to draw out," for she had drawn him out of the river, but God planned for Moses to draw His people out of their lives as slaves to the Egyptians.

Our children are God's before they are ours. Moses' mother had to literally give her baby into God's care. God had plans for her boy, and He has plans for your children too.

Think & Talk

How are you helping your children become who God created them to be?

Are you helping them discover God's dream for them? Or are you molding them into your dreams?

How can you help your children find and develop the God-given potential in each of them?

Fun Times with Younger Kids

Needed: plastic container, small doll

Make bath time part of your activity together. Include your children in a search for something to be the "basket." This could be a dairy topping plastic container or a disposable plastic bowl. Then find something to be the baby: a small doll, make a Lego® baby, or wrap a spoon in a handkerchief. The children can place the "Baby Moses" in the "basket" and re-enact the story while they take a bath.

Say: How do you think Moses' sister felt when she saw the princess pull the basket out of the water? God protected Baby Moses from the evil Pharoah.

Fun Times with Older Kids

Needed: sink full of water, rock

Say: Moses' mother knew if she put the baby in the basket and then put it in the river, the basket would take on water and sink. So she covered the basket with a substance like tar. No water could get into the basket, and the baby was safe.

Do a simple science experiment with your kids. Fill the kitchen sink with water. Now, drop a rock in the water. It sinks! That wasn't difficult. But what can you do to that rock to keep it from sinking? Without giving the kids any clues, see what they come up with. Here are some options (but don't be limited by these): set it in a margarine cup or put it in a sandwich bag full of air. How could a balloon, craft sticks, or play dough help keep the rock afloat? Each time you have an idea, check it in the sink full of water.

GOD PROTECTED BABY MOSES AND GOD PROTECTS US TOO.

Moses Becomes a Shepherd
[EXODUS 2:11-25]

Read "Moses Becomes a Shepherd" in your *Egermeier's® Bible Story Book*.

Story Background

Though he grew up in the highest levels of Egyptian society, Moses knew his background. When he left the shelter of the palace, he could see the great oppression the Israelites suffered. One day when he saw an Egyptian beating an Israelite, his anger boiled. He decided it was time to come to the rescue of his people. He took a very drastic step and killed the Egyptian, then buried him in the sand. The next day when he again went out to find ways to right the wrongs being done to the Israelites, he saw two of them fighting each other. When he broke up the fight, one of the Israelites asked Moses if he was going to kill him like he did the Egyptian the day before. Moses was cut to the quick by this question for two reasons: one, because he hoped the Israelites would see him as a hero working for them; and two, because this question let him know the murder he committed was not a secret. Not only had he failed to help his people, he had put himself in grave danger. He would soon be a wanted man.

IF WE DON'T CONTROL OUR ANGER, OUR ANGER WILL CONTROL US.

Moses' reaction was to run away and lose himself in the desert. There he found work as a shepherd for a man named Jethro. He married Jethro's daughter and began a family of his own, but Moses was a broken man. He had lost his position, his wealth, and his dream. Moses, an educated man, brought up as a prince in the center of the greatest civilization on earth, was now doing boy's work for his father-in-law in the middle of a barren desert. Did you catch all of that? Worst of all, he had lost his purpose. He had no hope of doing the work God had given him. He had made a terrible mess of his life, and for the next 40 years he lived as an utter failure. Moses chose the wrong method to do a great work.

When have you seen someone's best intentions turned into a big fiasco? (For example: a parent who works so much to provide nice things for his/her family that the family falls apart because he/she is not there to lead it.)

How can you guard against that happening to you?

How can you encourage someone who has tried his best and failed miserably?

Fun Times with Younger Kids

Needed: bag of marshmallows

Count out 20 marshmallows and then hide them around the house in places that are appropriate for the age and skill of your children.

Say: These marshmallows are white and fluffy like sheep. Sometimes, a sheep wanders away, and the shepherd has to go look for it. That's part of his job—to always know where his sheep are. Once the shepherd finds the sheep, he brings it back to the fold—the place where the sheep are kept together. That's what Moses was doing now. He had been a royal prince, and now he was a shepherd out in the desert.

Before beginning, each child needs to designate a particular place as the fold for the sheep they gather. At the signal, the kids will go in search of the marshmallows. Each time they find a marshmallow "sheep," they must return it to the fold before finding another one.

Fun Times with Older Kids

Needed: 10 disposable cups

Say: When the seven daughters came to water their sheep, they had some trouble. What was the trouble? Other shepherds tried to drive the daughters' sheep away. Moses stepped in to help them, and that's what started his new relationship with Jethro—his soon to be father-in-law.

JESUS IS OUR GOOD SHEPHERD. READ JOHN 1:1-18. HOW DOES JESUS TAKE CARE OF US LIKE A SHEPHERD?

37

Set the 10 cups across one wide end of a room to represent the sheep. One person will be "Moses," standing in front of the cups (sheep) to protect them. Two other family members will try to grab a cup without Moses tagging them. Keep switching roles…and have fun!

Moses and the Burning Bush
[EXODUS 3-4]

Read "Moses and the Burning Bush" in your *Egermeier's® Bible Story Book.*

Story Background

If you spent many days alone in the desert, you would not think it unusual to see something that wasn't really there; however, Moses saw a strange thing that just didn't go away. Finally, he realized it was not a mirage, but a bush on fire on top of the mountain. Now 80 years old, and having spent the last 40 years in the desert, Moses probably thought he had seen about all there was to see in the wasteland. As he approached the bush, he noticed that though it was burning, the fire did not consume it. As if that wasn't strange enough, a Voice came out of the bush.

God spoke to Moses from the bush and instructed him to go into Egypt to bring His people out of slavery and oppression. You might think Moses would jump for joy. This was exactly what he had wanted and tried to do in his youth. But 40 years of living as a failure had changed Moses. Perhaps that was necessary to make him humble enough to submit to God's plan.

God had a difficult time convincing Moses that he was the right man for this mission. After God gave Moses three signs to convince the Israelites God had sent him, then God shared His true name with Moses. This had never happened before! The name of God is YHWH, or Yahweh. It means I AM! God is not merely the God of Abraham, Isaac, and Jacob; He is the God of Moses, and He is *our* God. Notice, I AM is in the present tense. God is not the God of the past. His name is not I WAS. He is not simply the God of the future: I WILL BE. He is here and now, wherever and whenever the here and now happen to be. He is I AM!

WHAT ARE SOME OTHER NAMES FOR GOD? USE A CONCORDANCE OR COMPUTER TO FIND THEM.

Yahweh promised to be present with Moses as he confronted Pharaoh and led His people. Moses was afraid, as well he might be, but God was with him. This same God promises to be with you as you live your life and do His mission for you. Do not be afraid. Yahweh (I AM!) is with you.

Think & Talk

What frightens you about the future? About the present? Ask God to make His presence known as you face it with Him.

TURN YOUR FEAR OVER TO GOD.

Make it a practice to say to yourself, "I AM is with me." With that thought in your heart and head, this great assurance will be part of you when challenges arise.

Fun Times with Younger Kids

Needed: very small items

Say: God asked Moses, "What's that in your hand?" What was in Moses' hand? It was his rod. What did God tell Moses to do with his rod? He told him to throw it down. What happened when Moses threw it down? It turned into a snake.

Gather some very small items from around the house: penny, paper clip, rubber band, piece of candy, dried bean, macaroni. Make sure each thing can be held inside your child's hand when he or she makes a fist. Lay all the items out where you can see them. While everyone has their eyes closed, the child will pick one item and put it in his or her hand, then choose a family member to guess what it is. Each time, everyone will say together, "What's that in your hand?"

Fun Times with Older Kids

Needed: large pieces of paper, markers

Say: When Moses asked God what he was supposed to say if the Israelites asked who had sent him, God told Moses to respond that I AM sent him. God said that His name is I AM.

Provide some large pieces of paper and markers to make a banner together. This is not an assignment for your child, but something for you to do together. Be mindful to continue the conversation as you draw. The heading of the banner should be in huge letters, I AM. Then draw pictures or write about God to complete the sentence, "I am…." (For example: I am King of Kings. I am merciful. I am Creator.) As things come to mind later in the week, they can be added to the banner. Then post it somewhere in your house or garage where you'll see it regularly.

The Death Angel
[EXODUS 11:1–13:19]

Read "The Death Angel" in your *Egermeier's® Bible Story Book.*

Story Background

THE 10 PLAGUES
BLOOD
FROGS
GNATS
FLIES
LIVESTOCK
BOILS
HAIL
LOCUSTS
DARKNESS
DEATH OF
FIRSTBORN

Moses met with Pharaoh several times to seek the release of the Israelites. Each time Pharaoh refused to permit the Israelites to go into the wilderness to offer sacrifices and worship God. Each time God sent a plague to Egypt to demonstrate His power to Pharaoh, but Pharaoh would not change his mind. Finally, God sent this most terrible plague: the death of the firstborn. Pharaoh not only permitted the Israelites to leave, but he actually ordered them out. That last night in Egypt became the most celebrated night in Judaism.

That evening's events were packed with symbols, which became very important to the Israelites as they celebrated each year from then on. The symbol of the blood is still relevant to Christians even 4,000 years later. The blood of the lamb placed over the door saved the Israelites from the death angel and the slavery of Egypt. The blood of the Lamb of God, Jesus, saves us from the slavery of sin. That night, and the events that followed, are fundamental to Judaism. Time and again this night is revisited in the Old Testament, particularly in the Psalms.

In the New Testament, the fundamentals of Christianity are the crucifixion and resurrection of Jesus. God chose a Passover weekend to help people make the connection between past events (the Passover and the salvation of the Israelites) and what would happen in the future (the shedding of Jesus' blood and the salvation of the souls of all people).

The Lord sent the death angel to do for the Israelites what they could not do for themselves: free them from the oppression of the Pharaoh. In the same way, Jesus did for us what we could not do for ourselves: He freed us from the oppression of Satan. Freedom was won at the Passover. The Israelites only had to follow Moses through the wilderness to claim it. Freedom from sin was won for us at Calvary. We only have to follow Christ throughout our lives to claim it. He did for us what we could not do for ourselves. We do for Him the things we can.

Think & Talk

Are you allowing something to keep you in slavery—to keep you from being free? Identify what it is and why you continue living with something else controlling you.

Have you trusted in the promise of Christ's blood on the cross? What has He freed you from?

What wilderness are you going through, or have you gone through? How can you confidently follow Him through it?

Fun Times with Younger Kids

Needed: apple, 2 t. lemon juice, ¼ c. chopped nuts, 2 T. brown sugar, 1 T. honey, ¼ t. cinnamon, bowl, spoon, knife

Say: God instructed the Israelites to be ready to leave at a moment's notice. He even wanted them to eat a special meal and eat it standing up! One of the dishes from that meal is called charoset (or haroseth). It's easy to make and really yummy! The haroseth was supposed to remind the Israelites of the bricks and mortar they had to make for Pharoah's buildings.

Make some haroseth with your children. Peel one apple and core it. Let the child cut it up into tiny pieces…tiny, tiny pieces…keep chopping. Put the chopped apple in a bowl and then toss it with 2 t. lemon juice. (You can also use orange, grape, or any juice you have.) Chop ¼ cup of nuts very fine and add those to the apples. Add 2 T. brown sugar, 1 T. honey, and ¼ t. cinnamon. Then, stir it well. Enjoy sharing your haroseth with one another!

THE WORD "CHAROSET" IS FROM THE HEBREW LANGUAGE AND MEANS "CLAY."

Fun Times with Older Kids

Needed: oil, honey, salt, eggs, water, flour, sea salt, mixer, rolling pin, pizza cutter, cooking untensils

Say: The bread the Israelites made did not have any leaven in it. That's because it takes hours for the yeast (leaven) to cause the bread to rise, and they did not have time to wait. God told them to be ready to leave Egypt that very night. So, the bread was more like a thick cracker. Would you like to make some unleavened bread together? It's a fun project for the whole family!

In a large mixing bowl, combine: ¼ c. oil, ¼ c. honey, 2 t. salt, 3 eggs, and 1½ c. water. Mix these well and then add 4 c. flour. Mix and knead until you have a stiff dough. Divide the dough into 3 parts. Lightly flour the kitchen counter and roll each piece to the thickness of a pie crust (or thinner). Use a pizza cutter to cut the large piece of dough into squares. Place the squares on a greased cookie sheet and prick them with a fork. Sprinkle the pieces with sea salt. Bake in a preheated 375° oven for 10 minutes (or until lightly browned).

Food for Hungry Travelers
[EXODUS 16]

Read "Food for Hungry Travelers" in your *Egermeier's*® *Bible Story Book*.

Story Background

The desert of the Sinai Peninsula is a forbidding place. Some estimates say that Moses was leading 600,000 people. When the food they brought with them from Egypt ran out, they faced mass starvation. The hopeless specter of hunger made them forget how terrible their situation in Egypt had been. They complained that Moses had led them to this terrible place to die, and they wanted to go back to their former lives.

God provided for them in spite of their complaining. A huge flock of quail appeared from nowhere for a tasty feast. In addition, God provided a daily supply of a mysterious substance called manna. No one knows exactly what it was, but it supplied the people's need as long as the need continued. Manna could not be stored and quit appearing when more traditional food supplies were restored.

One of the most difficult assignments Moses tackled was turning a race of slaves into a race of conquerors. Life in Egypt was unpleasant, but the people's basic needs were met. The Sinai desert was a place of total desolation, and they would have died if not for the Lord's help. The Israelites had forgotten that their lives in Egypt began as an effort to escape famine. Four hundred years earlier God had provided for Jacob's family when Joseph was Pharaoh's prime minister. They didn't realize that God would provide again for them in the desert when He called them out of Egypt to return to claim their Promised Land in Canaan.

It's the same for us. When God calls us to do something for Him, He will take care of us. His call is not a guarantee of ease; instead, it is a guarantee of purpose and provision. Just as the

THE SINAI DESERT COVERS OVER 23,000 SQUARE MILES.

Israelites had to adjust their appetites to manna and quail, sometimes we must adjust our expectations to be able to do what God leads us to do. Some things in our lives might change (like finances, hobbies, the neighborhood where we live, the amount of time we watch television) when we commit to follow Him. Following Him might mean that we begin to lead a Bible study, mentor a child in reading, become a missionary, provide meals for those recovering from surgery, work with drug addicts, sit on a leadership board, repair a single mom's car, pastor a church, or give more money. God will provide. As He enabled the Israelites, He will enable us.

Think & Talk

Has God challenged you to do something for Him that you have put on hold? List some of the possibilities right now.

Was putting it on hold your idea or His? What would give you the assurance to move on?

What step can you take that will show you trust God to provide what you need? How will you share this with your children? What will you teach them through your journey with the Lord?

Fun Times with Younger Kids

Needed: small yellow balloons, black permanent marker

Blow up a bunch of small yellow balloons. With a black permanent marker draw 2 eyes and a beak on each balloon. Now, place the balloons all over the house.

Say: When the Israelites complained that they were hungry, God gave them two things: quail (little birds) and manna (a white, flaky substance). All they had to do was go out and pick it up for that day's food. It's time to find your quail for today!

The kids will run around the house, locating the yellow balloon quail. Each time they find a quail, they must return it to the starting area before looking for another one. Incorporating this one instruction of "returning before looking for another" is a great exercise for preschoolers as they are learning order and following directions.

Needed: small crackers (like Wheat Thins®), plate, small caps, small cookie cutters

Say: The Israelites complained to Moses that they were hungry. Because they were wandering around the desert, they didn't have the same foods they had when they were slaves in Egypt. They had forgotten how difficult life was as a slave. God provided 2 types of food for them: quail (little birds) and manna (white, flaky substance). They must have come up with lots of different ways to use the manna.

Give each person at least 6 small crackers.

Say: Let's see how many ways we can come up with to serve these little crackers.

Look through the cabinets and refrigerator to come up with different toppings or ways to serve the crackers. You're making an appetizer smorgasbord! You can also use small caps or cookie cutters to make the toppings more decorative. Different toppings might include: jelly, peanut butter, chocolate sauce, squirt cheese, bologna, hot dogs, sliced cheese, cream cheese, cereals. Use the small caps or cookie cutters on lunchmeats, breads, or cheeses.

Set all the new creations on a plate for a taste test and see which ones you like best.

WHAT FOODS WOULD YOU MISS MOST IF YOU ONLY HAD QUAIL AND MANNA TO EAT?

Crossing the Red Sea
[EXODUS 13:20–15:21]

Egermeier's **Bible Story Time**

Read "Crossing the Red Sea" in your *Egermeier's® Bible Story Book.*

Story Background

The Israelites left the civilized world of Egypt to go to the Promised Land. They knew the Promised Land was Canaan, but none of them had been there. More than 400 years had passed since Jacob's family had moved to Egypt. Moses knew the wilderness, but there is no evidence that he had been anywhere near Canaan. The thrill of being set free was soon tempered with the vast, barren land that stretched before them. The wilderness was a very hot, extremely dry, rocky desert. To leave the green valley of the Nile and face the seemingly endless expanse of nothing would soon become daunting. God provided a cloud by day and a pillar of fire at night to guide their way. They could not explain either, but they learned to follow them, and became less fearful.

THE RED SEA IS ABOUT 220 MI. WIDE AND AN AVERAGE OF 1,608 FT. DEEP. ITS GREATEST DEPTH IS 7,254 FT.

The fear hit them again full force, however, after the cloud led them to the shore of the Red Sea and reports came that Pharaoh's army was after them. Panic arose until Moses told them to *stand still, and see the salvation of the Lord* (Exodus 14:13, KJV). Then Moses raised his staff, the Red Sea parted, and God made a way of escape for them. When Pharaoh's army followed, they were totally destroyed.

The lesson for us is that when there seems to be no way to move forward, don't panic. Instead, stand still, quiet yourself, and watch what God is going to do. Sometimes, He provides a miracle that enables us to go on as before, and other times He provides a miracle by making us able to endure.

Have you ever wondered if God had abandoned you? When have you seen Him provide a way you could not foresee out of a bad situation?

What do you need to do to be able to stand still when you are up against your Red Sea? Do you need the strength to take the way out or to endure where you are? Ask God for eyes to see Him at work and the power to do your part.

Fun Times with Younger Kids

Needed: paper dessert plates, stapler, dried beans or small pasta, markers, spoon

Say: When the Israelites got to the other side of the Red Sea, they celebrated. Moses wrote a song and everyone danced. Some of the people played instruments like tambourines. They must have had a great time celebrating!

Each person will decorate the bottoms of two dessert paper plates using markers. Make a tambourine by putting the plates top-to-top. Kids can help push down on the stapler as you put staples around three-fourths of the edge. This will leave an opening to add dried beans and/or pasta. (The staples need to be almost touching one another.) Pour in 5 spoonfuls of dried beans or small pasta. Then, staple the open space completely.

Turn on some music and dance along with your children to celebrate God's goodness…just like Moses and the Israelites.

Fun Times with Older Kids

Needed: ping-pong balls, glasses of water

Say: What did you find most amazing about this story? How do you think the people felt when they came to the edge of the Red Sea and couldn't get across? How do you think they felt when the waters parted and there was a dry path across? How do you think they felt when they were out in the middle of the Red Sea with walls of water on both sides?

In June 2011, Penny Palfrey set the record for the longest solo unassisted ocean swim. She swam 70 mi. in 40 hrs. and 41 min.

We're going to play a game of getting across the Red Sea. Our water, though, is safely contained in some glasses! Two people will play at a time. Each player will need 6 glasses of water, so fill 12 glasses. Set glasses #1 and #2 about 3" apart on the floor. Set glasses #3 and #4 back at least 3 feet from the first 2 glasses and 3" apart. Set glasses #5 and #6 back a few more feet from #3 and #4 and 3" apart. Do this for both players. The object is for each player to blow a ping-pong ball between each set of glasses and to be the first one to get across the Red Sea with the ball.

Jethro Advises Moses
[EXODUS 18]

Bible Story Time

Read "Jethro Advises Moses" in your *Egermeier's® Bible Story Book*.

Story Background

Moses had returned to the desert, leading a great crowd of Hebrews. He was more than a leader; he was their only government. When Jethro, his father-in-law, visited him, Moses was overwhelmed with the job of governing 600,000 people in the middle of nowhere. Not only did they have the extraordinary problems of finding food and water, but they also had the everyday disputes that so many people generate. Jethro gave Moses the wise advice to delegate the administration of the people. He told Moses to tackle the big things, seeking God's direction and teaching God's law, and to find others to take care of the day-to-day problems that cropped up between individuals. As Moses shared leadership, more was accomplished and he didn't die of exhaustion.

Who is your Jethro? Do you have someone who can speak wisdom into your life? Moses had known Jethro for many years and trusted him. Do you have a friend that you trust like that? All of us need a coach or mentor who can help us get a better grasp on the situations we face. Perhaps you grew up in a tough situation, and you don't have a pattern to follow as you try to build a great family. Ask God to help you find someone who has built the kind of family you want yours to be and is willing to share his/her wisdom with you.

ALL OF US NEED A COACH OR MENTOR.

Moses had to trust those he appointed to serve under him. He had to know that though they might not do everything exactly like he would, they would get the job done. Moses accomplished God's dream for him because he didn't get bogged down doing things others could do and were called to do.

Think & Talk

What strategies do you use to stay on top of your responsibilities? Or are you feeling stuck?

When do you feel overwhelmed? Do you feel your responsibilities at home or work have become more than you can handle? Ask God to help you find ways to prioritize and delegate some of the responsibilities so you can concentrate on the areas that most need your attention.

Ask God to help you trust people to do what you need them to do. Delegation can range from giving chores to family members at home to making assignments at work.

Fun Times with Younger Kids

Needed: large bag of M&Ms®, bowl, 6 Lego® people

Say: Moses was working too hard, trying to answer the questions of all the people—600,000 people! That's a lot of people! His father-in-law, Jethro, told him that he should choose people who would take care of smaller groups of people.

Place the 6 Lego® people on the table. Pour the M&Ms® into a bowl. Take a blue M&M® and place it in front of one of the Lego® people. **Say:** This guy is going to be in charge of the blue M&Ms®. Put a green M&M® in front of a different Lego® person. **Say:** This guy is going to be in charge of all the green M&Ms®. Continue doing this with orange, red, brown, and yellow. Now, your preschooler will put all the M&Ms® with their correct Lego® man as quickly as he or she can.

Say: Moses got help by choosing some other men to help him take care of groups of people.

Fun Times with Older Kids

Needed: 3 balloons, timer

Blow up three balloons and tie them off. Choose someone to watch the time and signal to start. At the signal, one person will see how long he/she can keep all three balloons in the air without any of them touching the ground.

Say: How was this game like the situation Moses was in? Moses was trying to take care of everything and everybody. It was impossible to keep going like that! He couldn't keep all the balloons in the air…at the same time…all the time.

Now, give a balloon to three different people. At the signal, they will all keep their one balloon in the air.

Say: You were able to do it for a lot longer time this way, weren't you? Jethro advised Moses to divide up the responsibilities so that no one had too much. By doing that, everything would go smoother and the needs of the people would be taken care of.

The Golden Calf
[EXODUS 24:17-18, 32:1-35]

Egermeier's Bible Story Time

Read "The Golden Calf" in your *Egermeier's® Bible Story Book*.

Story Background

To get God's instructions, Moses climbed the mountain where he had seen the burning bush. The people promised to wait for him to return. When he didn't come back within the timeframe they thought he should, they became restless. They asked Moses' brother Aaron to supply them with a new god that would lead them, since apparently Moses was gone for good. The people knew God had planned to lead them to the Promised Land, but they were tired of waiting for Moses. Since they didn't have Moses to act as their representative with God, they decided to create their own god to take them to the Promised Land.

MT. SINAI, WHERE MOSES RECEIVED THE 10 COMMANDMENTS, WAS THE SAME PLACE HE HAD SEEN THE BURNING BUSH.

Aaron collected their gold and made a statue of a golden calf, which they began to worship. Just then Moses came down the mountain carrying the Ten Commandments God had given him. These commandments were meant to be the basis for the society the people would build in the Promised Land. Moses was so angry when he saw the golden calf and the people worshiping it, he forgot himself and threw down the tablets on which the commandments were written. He melted down the calf and made the gold into powder; then he put the powder in their water and forced the people to drink it. Later, he went back up the mountain to ask God to give him the commandments again.

Sometimes, when we have a problem, God's timing is not what we expect or hope for. He is the boss, and He does things by His own timetable. The temptation is to try to help Him along. Often, that's when we get in trouble. We think we see the outcome God wants, and especially when it's the outcome we also want, we take things into our own hands to reach it. This is true with big decisions like: when, if, and whom to marry;

which career to pursue; whether or not to buy a house and which one to buy. When it comes to these decisions, we are tempted not to wait on God. We think we can speed things up and take some of the pressure off Him. This story shows that God neither needs us to speed Him up or to worry about how He handles pressure.

Think & Talk

In what area of your life are you waiting for God's answer?

How do you rate your patience?

Do you need faith because you think He may have forgotten your situation?

Tell Him your anxiety and instead of trying to "help" Him as the Israelites did, wait for Him to act or give you the green light.

Fun Times with Younger Kids

Needed: vanilla wafers or graham crackers, sandwich bag

Make an interesting snack. Give each kid 3 vanilla wafers or graham crackers.

Say: While Moses was away, the people brought their gold to Aaron and he put it all together to make a golden calf idol.

As you say this, take the wafers from the children one at a time and put them in a stack.

Say: When Moses came down from the mountain, he was angry by what he saw. He took the gold calf, crushed it, and then put the powder in their drinks.

Give each child a sturdy sandwich bag and their wafers back. Place the wafers in the bag and seal it securely. Now, let them figure out how to crush the wafers into dust. Some suggestions: use a rolling pin or meat tenderizer, stomp on them, or pound the bag with the back of a small pan. Everyone can eat their wafer dust right out of the bags!

METALLIC GOLD IS NOT POISONOUS, BUT NO ONE WOULD WANT IT IN A DRINK!

Fun Times with Older Kids

Needed: 3 empty pop cans, bowl of ice water, thick gloves, water

GOD WANTS
US TO
CRUSH SIN!

Say: Moses was super mad when he returned and saw that the people were worshipping a gold calf. So, what did he do? He destroyed the idol by CRUSHING it…pulverizing it into dust. Moses wasn't done, though. He took the gold dust and added it to their drinking water, so they had to drink it. Let's see what we can crush!

Add 2 tablespoons of water to each of 3 pop cans. Then set the cans on a burner of your stove. When you see steam coming from the cans, they are ready. An adult will put the glove on, grab one of the cans, and immediately turn it upside down into a bowl of ice water. As soon as the can hits the ice water, you'll hear a huge "POP!" and you'll probably jump a bit the first time. The pop was from the can being crushed. You'll want to do more than one can because it's just so much fun!

Say: Moses CRUSHED the golden calf idol!

The Twelve Spies
[NUMBERS 13–14]

Bible Story Time *Egermeier's*

Read "The Twelve Spies" in your *Egermeier's® Bible Story Book*.

Story Background

This story is about seeing things as God sees them and obeying Him. The twelve spies sent to check out the Promised Land saw its richness and knew that it would be a wonderful place for their families. They also saw that the people who were already there lived in walled cities and that many of the people were physically intimidating. Two of the spies, Caleb and Joshua, were raring to go take the land and make it their own, while the other ten spread fear among their people. Caleb and Joshua knew God would enable them to win the land. The vote was ten to two to retreat to their former life in Egypt. This was a case when the majority was wrong. The minority saw God's vision, and His vision trumps the fears and shortsightedness of the majority.

> "ONE ON GOD'S SIDE IS A MAJORITY."
> —WENDELL PHILLIPS

Ultimately, the generation that had lived in slavery would not be the generation that conquered and claimed the Promised Land. When Moses told them this and led them back into the wilderness, they rebelled and attacked the Promised Land on their own without Moses' leadership or God's blessing. They were badly beaten, and the Israelites returned to the desert. Forty years would pass before the next generation—the one raised in the wilderness and trained to be conquerors—would enter the land.

The ten spies saw themselves as grasshoppers compared to the people living in the land. They had a self-esteem problem and a faith problem. They couldn't see themselves winning, and they couldn't see their God winning either. Caleb and Joshua knew better, and they were the only people of their generation to enjoy the promise of God in the land.

Think & Talk

What is your reaction when there is a giant—a big challenge—in your way? Ask Him to give you the courage to face the giants in the way.

Ask God to give you His vision for yourself, for your family, and for your children.

Put yourself in His hands and ask Him to enable you to make His vision for you a reality.

Fun Times with Younger Kids

Choose four rooms of your house. In each room place something small that obviously does not go there, or is unexpected. (For example: a toaster on the nightstand in the bedroom.) Send the kids into the rooms with the assignment to SPY. They should return to tell you what they found that was unusual.

Say: The 12 spies went into the Promised Land and found some things that were unusual. Name some of the things that surprised them. The people were like giants and made the spies feel like little grasshoppers. Even the clusters of grapes were huge. They brought back grapes that took two men to carry on poles. How do you think you would feel?

Fun Times with Older Kids

Needed: small caps, purple craft paint, green marker, large sheet of white paper, disposable plate

JAPAN'S RUBY ROMAN GRAPES ARE ONE OF THE LARGEST GRAPES AROUND TODAY.

You'll need to find some small caps off of things like hair mousse, shampoo, mouthwash, or hand cream. (A communion cup also works well.) Squirt out a thin layer of purple craft paint on a disposable plate. Each family member will make their own huge bunch of grapes by dipping the end of the cap in the paint and then stamping a circle on the paper. Each circle is a grape, so add lots and lots of grapes! At the top, draw in some leaves with a green marker. The bunches of grapes the spies found were huge! Don't just set up your child for this project; sit down and make it along with them.

Say: Do you think you would've been more like the 10 spies who didn't want to go into the land, or would you have been like Joshua and Caleb? What do you think you would've said when you saw the huge grapes? What do you think you would've said when you saw that the people were "giants"? How can you be more like Joshua and Caleb?

The Brass Serpent
[NUMBERS 21:4-9]

Egermeier's **Bible Story Time**

Read "The Brass Serpent" in your *Egermeier's® Bible Story Book.*

Story Background

HEALING COMES WHEN WE OBEY GOD.

Life in the wilderness was very hard for the Israelites, but they managed to make it even worse for Moses by their constant complaining. Once again, they complained about the water and food situation. Again, they wanted to go back to slavery in Egypt instead of finishing the exodus. While they were griping about the situation, poisonous snakes found their way into the camp. Those who were bitten died. At God's instruction Moses made a brass snake and put it on a tall pole in the camp. Those who were bitten were healed if they looked at the serpent on the pole.

This story is of special interest because Jesus mentions it. In John 3:14-15 (NIV) Jesus says, *Just as Moses lifted up the snake in the wilderness, so the Son of Man must be lifted up, that everyone who believes may have eternal life in him.* Jesus often referred to himself as the "Son of Man." Here He was telling us that He would be lifted up on a pole—in His case a cross—and people would be healed from the deadly snakebite of sin if they looked to Him with their hearts.

We can take this one step further. In the Bible, particularly in Genesis, the serpent represents Satan and sin. In 2 Corinthians 5:21 (NIV) Paul says, *God made him who had no sin to be sin for us, so that in him we might become the righteousness of God.* Our perfect Savior, Jesus, took our sins on Himself on the cross… spiritually becoming like the snake on the pole…so we might be saved from the deadly bite of sin. Just as the bitten Israelites were healed when they looked at the snake on the pole, you and I can be saved from sin. Just as the natural consequence of being bitten by the poisonous snakes was death, so the natural consequence of our sin is eternal death. God did a healing miracle in the bodies of the Israelites with the snake on the pole, and He does a spiritual miracle in our souls when we trust in the crucified Christ.

Think & Talk

When did you look to Jesus for your forgiveness? Or is that something you have yet to do?

Are you dying from your sin, or are you receiving God's miracle of healing through Christ on the cross?

Confess your sins and believe the Lord took your sins on Himself on the cross, and you will be forgiven and live forever with Him. Sounds too simple, but it's true!

SALVATION IS A GIFT. READ 1 JOHN 1:9.

Fun Times with Younger Kids

Needed: chenille sticks (pipe cleaners), pencils, black marker

Curl the end of a chenille stick to form the head of a snake. Then wrap the rest of the chenille stick around the top half of a pencil.

Say: There were snakes coming into the camp and biting people. When the snakes bit the people, it caused them to get very sick and die. Each time the people looked up at the snake on the pole, they were made well.

Play with the chenille stick pencil. One person will raise and lower the pencil. Everyone else will lie on the floor or a couch. When the pencil is raised, then everyone will jump to their feet and say, "I'm healed!" Take turns raising the pencil. You can even do this as you watch TV together.

Fun Times with Older Kids

Needed: play dough, waxed paper/plastic placemat

Say: The snakebites were a punishment for all the complaining the Israelites were doing. What were they complaining about? What do you complain about? Do you complain at home? School? At work? To your friends? At church?

Each time someone shares something they have a habit of complaining about, he or she should make a play dough snake and lay it on a piece of waxed paper. Keep going until everyone has at least 3 "complaining" snakes.

Say: It's not enough to just acknowledge that we complain about some things. We need to do something about it! Taking a positive attitude, looking at things differently, or maybe just avoiding some situations are all ways to smash the complaining snakes.

Now, each person should share one way they can combat complaining about each thing they made a snake about. When they share, then they can smash that snake with their fist or the palm of their hand! (For a little extra fun, try smashing the snakes with different kitchen utensils, just to see what interesting shapes you get.)

Crossing the Jordan
[JOSHUA 3:1–5:12]

Read "Crossing the Jordan" in your *Egermeier's® Bible Story Book*.

Story Background

After 40 years in the wilderness, the Israelites were finally ready to cross into the land God had promised them. They had done more than wander during that time. While they traveled the desert, a transformation took place. They had fled Egypt and crossed the Red Sea as a race of slaves. Now, they were ready to cross the Jordan River as a race of conquerors. Joshua and the Israelites were on the brink of seeing the promise fulfilled that God made to Moses—the promise of a land flowing with milk and honey. Israel's wilderness experience would end in a similar way to its beginning—the people would miraculously pass through a body of water.

On the Canaan side of the Jordan, they found grain and abundant fruit growing. Those who had been born in the wilderness had been raised on the manna God provided each day. No one under the age of 40 had eaten anything made from grain. Imagine how they reveled in the bread and cakes, along with the fruit they could now enjoy!

Also on that day, God stopped providing the manna that sustained the Israelites in the desert. Instead, they had a fertile land to farm. The blessing of the manna was over. God continued to bless in a new way, even as the Israelites took responsibility to grow their own food.

This is a good thing for parents to remember. It is important for you to encourage, and sometimes even force, your children to take responsibility for themselves. Parents are successful when their adult children take care of themselves. As they grow, children need to assume responsibility appropriate to their age, so that when they are grown up, they truly are adults.

MANY YEARS LATER JOHN THE BAPTIST BAPTIZED JESUS IN THE JORDAN RIVER.

The Israelites might well have been satisfied to rely on manna forever, just as kids might be satisfied to let Mama and Daddy cook, clean and provide for them forever. In the wilderness, God prepared Israel for the Promised Land. During childhood, smart parents prepare children to be adults.

Think & Talk

How are you preparing your children to take responsibility for themselves?

What things do you need to stop doing for your child that he/she should be doing? (Parents need to agree on a strategy for preparing their children.)

Read Hebrews 5:13-14. How can this verse apply to helping your children move from one season of their lives to the next? Why is this a healthy thing?

Fun Times with Younger Kids

HAVE A SPECIAL FAMILY PRAYER TIME AROUND YOUR HANDMADE ALTAR.

Needed: plate, candle, match, rocks

Say: The Bible story you read told how Joshua had one man from each tribe gather a rock from the riverbed. What did they do with these rocks? They built an altar.

Take a walk to pick up some interesting rocks. Little ones absolutely love gathering rocks, sticks, and leaves! When you get home, place a candle in the middle of a plate. Then place the rocks that you gathered on the plate around the candle. You now have a family altar. Light the candle, turn down the lights, and pray together around your family altar.

Fun Times with Older Kids

Need: pool noodle, sharp knife, water, pitcher with a spout, paper

Say: The Israelites needed to cross the Jordan River, but getting across the muddy river was a problem. God did not stop the flow of water until the priests took one step into the river, believing God would provide a way as He said. Sometimes, we have to take a step of faith before God shows us how He is going to work. God stopped the flow of water, kind of like how a dam does…but without the dam. God is so amazing!

A parent will use a sharp knife to slice a pool noodle in half, lengthwise. Then, hold one end of the pool noodle slightly higher than the other end. Pour some water into the pool noodle trench at one end. Watch the water flow down the trench. This is like the water flowing down the Jordan River. Now, wad up some paper very tightly and plug the trench about halfway down the pool noodle. Pour the water again.

Say: What happens when the water gets to the paper wad? The water stops. That's what God did—He stopped the flow of the water. But God didn't need anything except His word to make the water stop.

The Israelites Settle in Canaan
(JOSHUA 13–19)

Egermeier's **Bible Story Time**

Read "The Israelites Settle in Canaan" in your *Egermeier's®*
Bible Story Book.

Story Background

THE ANAKITES
WERE THE
GIANTS
LIVING IN
THE PROMISED
LAND.

While there were still places where the original inhabitants
lived, the Promised Land was at last controlled by the Israelites.
The time had come for the army to go home. Joshua told each
tribe to finish the conquest of its own section of the land. At
that point an old hero reappeared—Caleb. Forty-five years
earlier, Caleb was one of the twelve spies Moses sent out before
the invasion. Of the twelve, only he and Joshua reported that
the Israelites could take the land. The others were so frightened
by the fortified cities and physical size of the Canaanites that
they caused the people's hearts to melt in fear. Courageously,
Caleb and Joshua declared that with the Lord's help the
inhabitants would be conquered and the land would belong to
God's people. Moses then promised Caleb that because of his
wholehearted faith and courage, he would possess the land he
had seen.

Now, at age 85, Caleb collected on that promise. He could have
chosen any of the land for his tribe, Judah. There was pastureland
and farmland galore, but Caleb chose the mountains where he
had seen the people described as giants. He declared himself
as strong and as ready to fight as he had been on the day he
made his report to Moses. Can't you see Caleb year after year
working out, chopping wood, training camels, or whatever
people did to keep themselves in shape in those days? At any
rate, he was still itching to fight those giants. The Lord had long
been with him, and Caleb still knew that with the Lord on his
side, no giants could stand in his way. So, the old warrior chose
the hill country where the giants lived as the inheritance for
him and his children. Caleb had learned to trust the Lord, and
he had kept his faith and body strong, ready for whatever God
wanted him to do.

Think & Talk

How can you keep yourself ready for the challenges in life that are before you?

How can you continue to grow in your faith in God so that when you are 85 you will be ready for the giants?

Fun Times with Younger Kids

Needed: cans of soup

Say: Even though Caleb was old, he had dreamed of the day when he would go back to the land where the giant people lived. The Bible tells us that he prepared himself for that day. He must've exercised and taken care of himself so that he would be strong when the time came. What kind of exercises do you think Caleb did?

Find some things around the house to use with exercises. For example, give everyone a can of soup and lift it up and down overhead to the beat of some music. Do chin-ups on a tree branch. Create an exercise for each room of the house. At the signal, everyone will run from room to room, doing the exercise the allotted number of times.

Fun Times with Older Kids

Needed: glass of water, quarters

Read Joshua 14:9.

Say: Why was Caleb given the land of Hebron—the land of the giants? It was because he had followed the Lord completely, all the days of his life…fully! Caleb had been faithful to the absolute limits.

Fill a glass to the very top, as full as it will go.

Say: Do you think this glass is all the way full?

Now, touch the edge of one quarter to the center of the surface of the water and gently let it drop into the water.

BE FAITHFUL TO THE MAX!

Say: Did the water overflow? No!

Drop another quarter into the water in the same manner. Add another 5 quarters.

Say: What has happened to the shape of the surface of the water? Does it look like it's stretching? Was the glass really full when we started? How is this like how Caleb was full of faith and fully committed to God? His faith was beyond what others thought possible.

Joshua's Farewell
[JOSHUA 23–24]

Bible Story Time *Egermeier's*

Read "Joshua's Farewell" in your *Egermeier's® Bible Story Book*.

Story Background

Joshua led the Israelites to victory, and though they did not occupy all the Promised Land, they dominated it and were working to complete the occupation. At the end of his life, Joshua gathered all the people together one more time. He recited the great works that God had done for them. From the appearance of Moses as their leader, to the escape from Pharaoh, to the long struggle in the wilderness, to crossing the Jordan River, to winning their place in the land, Joshua reviewed it all. Then he hit them with the clincher. Dramatically, he challenged them to make the choice. *Choose for yourselves this day whom you will serve, whether the gods your ancestors served beyond the Euphrates, or the gods of the Amorites, in whose land you are living. But as for me and my household, we will serve the Lord* (Joshua 24:15, NIV). The Israelites chose to accept his challenge, and for more than a generation, they kept their promise. But, this was a promise each generation must make for itself.

This same choice remains the challenge for you today. Will you decide to be like you were before you met Christ? Will you be like everyone else around you and seek whatever they seek—money, fame, status? Or will you serve the Lord and lead your family to do likewise?

WHAT DID JOSHUA TELL THE PEOPLE ABOUT GOD'S PROMISES?

READ JOSHUA 23:14.

Think & Talk

Take some time and write a personalized speech like Joshua's that fits your family. Include the answers to these questions in your declaration:

What has God done for you?

How have you seen His hand working in your lives to bring you to this point?

What challenges has He helped you overcome? What challenges do you need His help with today?

Can you say as Joshua did, *"As for me and my household, we will serve the Lord"*?

Write this proclamation and display it as a reminder that you have seen God working in you and your family and that you plan to stick with God no matter what. Make it something you and your children always remember and talk about. Live by it!

Fun Times with Younger Kids

Needed: building blocks, play figures

For this activity, you'll need Legos®, Lincoln Logs®, or something that you can build with. Build a home together that represents where your family lives.

Say: Who lives in your home? As you name each person, place a figure in the house to represent that person.

Say: Who is it that we cannot see, but who should be part of our home? God is the one everyone in our family should worship. We want to worship Him together.

Pull your child onto your lap in front of this little playhouse, and in short, simple sentences express to them that you will do your best to lead them as you all follow God together.

Say: Can we do this together?

Huddle together and put your hands on top of one another in the center.

Say: "As for me and my house, we will worship the Lord" and have the children repeat it after you. Then raise your hands in celebration!

Needed: stick-on letters, craft paint, paper plate, large piece of paper

Look up Joshua 24:15 and read it together out loud.

Say: This is a pledge our family can promise one another. It's not just for Joshua and his family. When we make a promise, it's nice to have it written down or have a reminder of it somewhere.

Spread a thin layer of craft paint on a paper plate. (It would be nice to have a different color of paint for each member of the family, but not necessary.) To symbolize that everyone has a part in this pledge, each person will press a hand in the paint and then firmly press that hand somewhere on the piece of paper. After the paint has dried, use the stick-on letters to write the scripture on the paper. Don't hesitate to put letters over the top of the handprints. (Date the back of the paper to make a nice keepsake.)

A PLEDGE IS A BINDING PROMISE OR AGREEMENT TO DO SOMETHING. IT HELPS HOLD EVERYONE ACCOUNTABLE.

Deborah Leads Israel
[JUDGES 4–5]

Read "Deborah Leads Israel" in your *Egermeier's® Bible Story Book*.

Story Background

After Joshua died, the Israelites eventually forgot their promise to serve only God. Trouble followed. With each trouble God raised up a hero—the Bible calls them "judges"—to lead the people out of the mess and bring them back to Him. These judges were strong leaders in battle; however, one of them was different from the rest because she was a woman: Deborah.

SISERA, THE COMMANDER OF THE CANAANITE ARMY, HAD 900 IRON CHARIOTS.

The people knew that God spoke through Deborah. When the Canaanites threatened the Israelites, she also emerged as a leader in battle. Her strategy trapped the much better armed Canaanites next to a bend in the river where their superior numbers and weapons were neutralized by the terrain. When the Canaanite leader, Sisera, fled, another brave woman, Jael, tricked him and assassinated him. For the next 40 years Israel was at peace.

In Old Testament times, women were considered second-class citizens. They did much of the real work, bore and reared the children, and often died young. Deborah must have been exceptional indeed for the Israelite men to ask for her advice and leadership. She did not let them, or the Lord, down.

Two things we can draw from the story of Deborah: First, don't be afraid to be the person God made you to be. Deborah didn't fit the classic role of an Israelite woman. She had surely endured ridicule and opposition in her life, but she persisted in speaking what God gave her to say. Eventually, she was called upon when she was needed. Second is a lesson from the male leader of Israel, Barak. He was known to be a brave soldier, but he was willing, even desirous, of having Deborah take the lead. When she pointed out that her presence in the battle would keep him from achieving fame, he still insisted she lead. The lesson here is that a true leader knows how to follow when that is the role God assigns him.

And a bonus third lesson from this story is from Sisera the Canaanite: don't drink milk and fall asleep in the tent of a woman you don't know!

Think & Talk

Are you learning to balance being both a leader and a follower? In your marriage? At work?

How can you help your children become both leaders and followers? If they have leadership abilities, give them opportunities to develop those, even at a very early pre-school age.

TRUE LEADERS KNOW WHEN AND WHO TO FOLLOW.

Fun Times with Younger Kids

Say: Sisera tried to hide from his enemies when he saw his army was in trouble. He found a tent that belonged to a woman named Jael. He thought he would be able to hide there, but he was wrong. Jael knew he was there, and she helped her people.

Preschoolers love, love, love to play "Hide and Seek." The funny thing is that they will hide in the same place over and over and think the results are going to be different. Playing "Hide and Seek" is a good time to review counting, taking turns, and waiting until it's time. The adults can make the search a little more challenging. If your child can't find you and starts to get upset, then call his or her name softly. It will reassure the child and allow him or her to follow the sound to discover you.

Fun Times with Older Kids

Needed: tennis racket, marble, green marker, Pez® dispenser

With a green marker, outline one little square on the tennis racket head. This square represents where Deborah sat under the palm tree. One person at a time will hold the racket out. Place a marble against the rim of the racket. By slightly tilting the racket, roll the marble until it rests in one of the squares touching the outlined square (Deborah). The marble represents someone coming to Deborah for advice. Play as long as you like.

Say: Why do you think so many people came to Deborah? She was a very wise woman, and everyone respected what she had to say. She always relied on God to help her know what to tell the people.

Now, hold out the Pez® dispenser.

Say: When you hold out your hand in front of the Pez® dispenser and someone tilts back the top, what happens? It dispenses candy, and we like that!

Dispense a piece of Pez® candy to everyone.

Say: When people came to Deborah, it was like they were holding out their hand for her advice, and Deborah dispensed it. She gave out the wise words of the Lord.

Gideon Attacks the Midianites

[JUDGES 7:1–8:28]

Bible Story Time

Read "Gideon Attacks the Midianites" in your *Egermeier's® Bible Story Book*.

Story Background

After 40 years of peace, the Israelites sinned again by worshiping idols and faced an invasion from a nomadic people, the Midianites. This time, God called on Gideon not only to lead the people and defeat the invaders but also to return to the Lord. Gideon gathered an army of 32,000, but God told him that was too large. God then directed Gideon to pare down the army to just 300 men.

God gave Gideon a brilliant plan of intrigue and deception. He actually used the Midianites themselves to bring about their own defeat. After the Israelites had an overwhelming victory, the Midianites left them alone. The success of the strategy led the Israelites to ask Gideon to be their king and start a ruling dynasty in Israel. Gideon declined; he knew the victory was the Lord's. God had appointed him leader for the confrontation with the Midianites, but God did not appoint Gideon king. Gideon would lead Israel as a judge for the rest of his life, but he never accepted the honor of being their king. He knew the popularity he had achieved among the people was solely for doing what God directed. Gideon wisely and humbly would take no more credit and no more reward than he deserved.

A great blessing is to see an accurate picture of who you are: your strengths, weaknesses, and capabilities. That's no easy task. The praise of people around you, as well as their ridicule, can distort the way you see yourself. Parents walk a tight rope with their children in this. They must be quick and constant with their encouragement. They must encourage their kids to reach for things that seem beyond the possible. At the same time, parents must help children deal with failure when it comes, and failure will most definitely come if the child honestly attempts

THE MIDIANITES WERE DESERT DWELLERS. AS NOMADS, THEY RAISED ANIMALS, MOVING FROM PLACE TO PLACE, AND MADE THEIR LIVING AS CARAVAN TRADERS AND BANDITS.

75

to excel in new things. Everyone finds things they just aren't good at when they are searching for who they are and what they were meant to do.

GOD HAS A PLAN.

READ JEREMIAH 29:11.

Think & Talk

How, and how often, are you encouraging your child to try new things?

How do you react when your child fails? Are you able to comfort him/her? Are you able to help your child accept the need to try something else?

Do you regularly remind your kids that God has something He wants them to do with their lives? How?

Fun Times with Younger Kids

Needed: small flashlights

Say: Gideon and his men had strange weapons! They used horns and torches to fight their enemy!

Kids love to play with flashlights! Give each child a flashlight that is easy to turn on and off. If you don't have one, dollar stores carry little ones that are perfect for preschoolers. This activity is especially fun after sundown. Each time you turn out the light in the room, say, "Toot-toot-toot-toot!" The kids will turn on their flashlights and echo back, "For Gideon and for the Lord!"

Fun Times with Older Kids

Needed: sandwich bags, trail mix

Say: God kept telling Gideon to send more men home. Which men did he tell to go home?

Use a snack to help reinforce the story. Give each child a serving of trail mix or a cereal mix in a sandwich bag. Choose one of the items in the bag for the kids to pull out and eat.

Say: I don't want you to have any almonds in your bag, so eat them right now.

Choose another item and do the same thing.

Say: I don't want you to have any Cheerios® in your bag, so go ahead and eat them.

Continue doing this until there is just one ingredient left in their bags.

Say: What does this story tell you about how God works? Gideon didn't think he was the best choice to lead the people in battle. When have you thought that you aren't big enough, or smart enough, or fast enough, or strong enough? What can you learn from how God used Gideon?

Samson Dies

[JUDGES 16:21-31]

Egermeier's **Bible Story Time**

Read "Samson Dies" in your *Egermeier's® Bible Story Book*.

Story Background

Samson was the Old Testament's version of a super-hero. He was a tremendous physical specimen with amazing courage. From birth he had been dedicated to the Lord's service. As part of his vow to be God's man, he did not cut his hair.

A NAZARITE WAS A PERSON WHO VOWED TO BE SET APART FOR GOD'S USE.

Even though he was a great hero, Samson disobeyed God by loving a Philistine woman. By doing so, he put himself at risk. She was persuaded to find out the source of Samson's strength and report it to her countrymen, the Philistines. His strength was in the Lord and in the vow he had made to God, symbolized by his long hair. When the Philistines cut his hair, Samson's strength dried up, they took him captive, blinded him, and forced him to do a donkey's work, pushing a grindstone. Finally, at a festival the Philistines decided to bring out the former superstar to make fun of him. Little did they know that while he had slaved at the stone, his faith had regrown along with his hair. Samson literally brought the house down on 3,000 Philistines and himself when he pushed down the support pillars he was standing between.

From Samson we learn that being unfaithful to the Lord has consequences. Samson got into trouble when he disobeyed the Lord. We also learn that it is possible to come back from a terrible mistake. Samson died the hero he had been before his fall. Finally, we learn that God can use us when we return to Him. We may not return to the same situation, but God always has a plan.

Think & Talk

Are you dealing with a temptation that could get you into real trouble? Name it and ask God for strength to overcome it.

What consequences of sin are you dealing with? Ask God to forgive you and help you rebuild what you have broken, or give you a fresh start.

Are you in the process of rebuilding your life after a disaster? Ask God for wisdom and strength to avoid making the same mistake again.

WHAT DOES THE BIBLE SAY ABOUT GOD'S FORGIVENESS?

READ DANIEL 9:9 & MATTHEW 6:14-15.

Fun Times with Younger Kids

Needed: 3 cardboard boxes, blindfold

Say: Because Samson disobeyed God, he lost his strength and his enemies caught him. They did terrible things to him. They treated him like an animal, and they blinded him. Samson could not see anymore, but he asked God to give him back his strength one last time. God gave him strength, and Samson pushed the pillars down on his enemies.

Blindfold one person. Then, very quietly set the 3 cardboard boxes on top of one another. The blindfolded person must find the box tower and knock it over. When the tower goes over, yell, "Samson got his strength back!"

Fun Times with Older Kids

Needed: rubber bands, 8 empty pop cans

Say: Samson lost his strength because he didn't keep his promise to God. His broken promise caused him a lot of pain and suffering. Samson knew he had done wrong, and he asked God to forgive him. Even though his hair grew out again, his amazing strength didn't come back. When Samson was being held prisoner, what special request did he make to God? He asked to have his strength restored one more time, so he could bring the pillars down on the people who mocked God.

Build two towers with the empty pop cans—4 cans stacked on top of one another for each tower. Stand back about 6 feet and take turns shooting rubber bands at the towers to see who can make them fall. Each time a tower falls, yell, "Way to go, Samson! Way to go, God!"

Ruth Goes with Naomi
(RUTH 1:1–19)

Egermeier's **Bible Story Time**

Read "Ruth Goes with Naomi" in your *Egermeier's® Bible Story Book.*

Story Background

THE TRIP TO
BETHLEHEM IS
ESTIMATED TO
HAVE TAKEN
7–10 DAYS
ON FOOT AND
INVOLVED
CLIMBING
OVER RUGGED
TERRAIN.

What a sad story…. Naomi's husband died; then her sons died. Due to the change in circumstances that originally brought Naomi to Moab, she now was able to return to Bethlehem. She was going home. How many times over the years had she dreamed of going home? But not like this. The only family she had left was her foreign daughters-in-law. She knew that life in Bethlehem would be at least as hard and lonely for them as life in Moab had been for her. Twice she told them to stay in Moab and find new husbands. The second time, Orpah took her advice, but Ruth continued the journey with Naomi.

In one of the Bible's most touching moments, Ruth pledged to go wherever Naomi went, make Naomi's people her own and Naomi's God her God. Today that pledge of love and loyalty is often quoted or sung in wedding ceremonies as the bride and groom vow to trek through life together. Making a marriage last a lifetime takes this kind of commitment.

The most amazing part of the story, however, is that Ruth is a widow, pledging loyalty to her widowed mother-in-law. Ruth chose to be the person Naomi could count on. How much more should a husband and wife make this pledge to each other. If married couples would live this way, we would have far fewer divorces and a lot more 50th wedding anniversaries.

Think & Talk

How are you incorporating Ruth's pledge into your marriage?

The best way to teach your children to be loyal to their future spouses is to be loyal to each other.

Life and relationships have ups and downs. Is your devotion to each other strong enough to endure whatever comes? If not, ask God together to make it so.

Fun Times with Younger Kids

Needed: tray, items that keep things together, dish towel

Put together a tray of items such as: scotch tape, duct tape, stapler, paper clip, safety pin, bottle of glue, stick of glue, zipper, chewing gum, magnet, shoestring, button, and a nail. Show the items to your children for about 30 seconds; then cover the tray. Take turns naming one of the items that was on the tray AND what it holds together. For example: a zipper; it holds together both sides of my jacket so the cold air doesn't get in.

Say: All of these items hold things together. Ruth and Naomi weren't held together with a zipper or a piece of duct tape. They were held together by love. Ruth wanted to go with Naomi because she loved her and didn't want to be separated from her. Who do you love and don't want to be away from?

LOVE HOLDS PEOPLE TOGETHER!

Fun Times with Older Kids

Needed: old strips of sheeting

Say: Ruth stuck with Naomi. Ruth told Naomi that she was going to go wherever Naomi went and live wherever she did. Naomi wasn't going to lose Ruth!

This activity resembles a 3-legged race. Tie the left leg of one person to the right leg of another person with 3 strips of old sheeting. While tied together in this way, accomplish a chore such as: wash the dishes, vacuum the carpet, make the beds, take the garbage cans to the street, or rake leaves.

Say: Why was that fun? What was difficult about it? How did you have to work together to get the chore accomplished? Ruth and Naomi worked together. Ruth went out and found places to pick up grain. Then she brought it back for Naomi to use to make their meal.

Boaz Marries Ruth
[RUTH 3—4]

Egermeier's Bible Story Time

Read "Boaz Marries Ruth" in your *Egermeier's® Bible Story Book*.

Story Background

A GODLY
CHARACTER
LASTS LONGER
THAN GOOD
LOOKS.

Ruth likely thought that by going to Bethlehem she was giving up her chance to remarry. She had taken on the responsibility of caring for her mother-in-law, Naomi, which might well prove to be a task a potential husband would want no part of. On top of that, she was a Moabitess. Even though she had left her old gods behind and had embraced Naomi's God, finding a good man who would take a foreign wife would not be easy.

Then Ruth met Boaz and, with Naomi's encouragement, attracted his attention. The custom in those days, which seems very odd in modern times, was that the male relative closest to a dead husband was automatically first in line to be the next husband of the widow. Boaz was a close relative, but not close enough. To marry Ruth he had to get the permission of the closer cousin. Ruth had impressed Boaz. Though she got him to notice her, she obviously had not chased after a mate. She was a respectable, hardworking woman who kept her promises. Ruth may well have been a physically attractive woman, but her looks were not what sold Boaz on her. He was impressed with who Ruth was inside: her integrity, her courage, and her modesty. (By the way, Ruth later gave Boaz a son, Obed, who fathered Jesse—the father of Israel's great king David, and a human ancestor of Jesus.)

The girls of our highly sexualized culture desperately need the lesson of Ruth. She attracted the best husband in town, not because she was drop dead gorgeous or because she tantalized him sexually. She won Boaz because she was a strong woman of good character. For Boaz, as for many men these days, it was not hard to find a good-looking woman, but it was and *is* difficult to find a woman with Ruth's character.

Think & Talk

How are you teaching your daughters that there is more to being attractive than becoming physically mature and alluring to boys?

How are you helping your sons see that there is more to a girl than the way she looks on the outside?

What are you teaching your children to look for in a mate?

Fun Times with Younger Kids

Needed: cornmeal, rice cereal, small bucket

Mix a good amount of cornmeal with some rice cereal in a small bucket.

Say: When Ruth went out to Boaz' field each day, she searched the ground to find little grains that the workers had missed. She and Naomi used the grain to make bread, so they would have food to eat. It was hard work! Boaz told his workers to leave extra for Ruth, so it wouldn't be so difficult for her.

Take turns looking through the cornmeal for the pieces of rice cereal. Your little ones will love finding the cereal treasures in the cornmeal. Enjoy the snack as you discover the grain!

Fun Times with Older Kids

Needed: waxed paper, bottle of glue, red food coloring, glitter

Say: What shape reminds you of love? It's the heart! Where did you hear about love in this story? Boaz and Ruth loved one another and got married. Ruth also loved Naomi and took care of her. Love keeps people together. Love sticks to you!

Make a special heart out of something that sticks things together—glue. Add a few drops of red food coloring to a bottle of glue until you have a strong pink color. On the waxed paper, squirt a thin outline of a heart about 3" in size. Then, give the bottle of glue to your child to finish squirting until the inside of the heart is filled in. (The best way to do this is to squirt some dots throughout the heart and then let it set a few seconds to see how it smooths out.) When it is completely filled in, then your child can sprinkle glitter into the top of the glue heart. Set this aside for a couple of days to dry completely. You'll then be able to peel the heart from the waxed paper and put it just about anywhere!

⭐ Bonus Activity:

Say: Ruth gathered grain, probably barley, which provided the food they lived on. She and Naomi very well may have made cakes like these.

HAVE A MEAL LIKE RUTH AND NAOMI MAY HAVE EATEN.

Make some pancakes using barley, so you can actually taste the earthy difference of barley flour.

1 c. white flour
1½ c. barley flour
1 egg, beaten
1 c. milk
1 T. vegetable oil
4 t. baking powder
pinch of salt

Mix all the dry ingredients together. Stir in the milk, egg, and oil. Drop onto a medium heat griddle. Wait until the raw side gets a little dull and then flip. The cake is done when both sides are golden brown. Add a little butter and syrup, and you've got some yummy pancakes!

The Ark of God Is Captured
[1 SAMUEL 3:19–4:22]

Bible Story Time *Egermeier's*

Read "The Ark of God Is Captured" in your *Egermeier's® Bible Story Book*.

Story Background

The Ark of the Covenant was a box encased in gold with two angels on the lid. Since the days of Moses, it had contained the tablets of the Ten Commandments, a jar of manna, and Aaron's rod. It was a kind of keepsake box for God's people. The Ark of the Covenant went before the armies of Joshua, across the Jordan River and into battle as they invaded Israel. The Ark represented the presence of God and was kept in the Holy of Holies in the tabernacle at Shiloh, where it had been for many years.

SHILOH WAS CONSIDERED THE CAPITAL CITY OF ISRAEL BEFORE THE TEMPLE WAS BUILT IN JERUSALEM.

By the time of Eli, the high priest, Israel had drifted far from God and had begun to worship idols. The people began treating the Ark as if it were an idol—like they thought God lived in it. When the Philistines defeated them, the Israelites decided to carry the Ark into battle, thinking it would magically give them victory. The Ark had led their ancestors to victory because God was with them, and the battle was His idea. Eli's sons thought taking the Ark would somehow force God to help them in battle; however, this particular battle with the Philistines was *their* idea, not God's. They learned that day that God will not be led by men. God didn't go with Israel, and Israel consequently lost the battle. Eli's sons were killed, but an even more devastating consequence was that the Ark was lost to the Philistines for a time.

Think & Talk

Keeping things to remind us of what God has done can help us pass the story of God's activity to new generations. Do you have a keepsake that represents a significant spiritual experience that you can share with your kids?

Things, even religious things that symbolize the Lord, can become idols when we put faith in them instead of God. When we keep things to remind us of the great things God has done, they should do just that—remind us of God.

God is never our servant. He is God, and we were designed to serve Him. We cannot order Him around. It is important not to get confused about this. We can ask God for anything, but we must trust that God loves us and will give us what is best for us, even if His decision is sometimes difficult to accept.

Fun Times with Younger Kids

Needed: small stuffed animal

Say: The Israelites had the Ark of the Covenant, a very special box, and the Philistines captured it. What does "capture" mean? The Philistines grabbed it and took it away where the Israelites couldn't get to it. Say, "capture." If I grabbed one of your toys and took it away where you couldn't find it, then you could say that I captured your toy.

Place a small stuffed animal on the floor. In the first round, a parent will stand on one side of the stuffed animal, about 2-feet back from it, as the guard. (You may want to put something on the floor to indicate where to stand.) Then, other family members will attempt to "capture" the stuffed animal by grabbing it. The stuffed animal is considered captured when someone successfully grabs it and pulls it to his/her chest before being tapped on the arm or hand by the guard. After the kids get the idea of how to guard the stuffed animal, switch the positions.

Fun Times with Older Kids

Needed: shoeboxes, art supplies

Say: The Ark of the Covenant was a keepsake box for the entire Israelite nation. God told Moses to place three specific items of importance in the Ark: the Ten Commandments tablets, a jar of manna, and Aaron's rod. Why do you think these three things were special for the Israelites to remember?

If you have a box of keepsakes, bring it out and share the stories behind some of the items. Explain that each thing you've kept is to remind you of someone or an experience that was very important to you. Some of the keepsakes probably have great monetary value, but most keepsakes would be trash to other people.

Decorate shoeboxes with paper, markers, and any other glue-on craft supplies you might have. Encourage your child to make this his/her own with pictures, designs, and colors that express a little about who they are. Once the box is done, decide on one or two items that will be placed there. These might be a special photo, a competition ribbon, the topper off a birthday cake, or the collar of a pet that is no longer with the family. As your child places the objects in the new keepsake box, listen closely as he/she shares the story that makes it a significant object.

KEEPSAKES REMIND US OF IMPORTANT EVENTS AND PEOPLE IN OUR LIVES, BUT THEY DO NOT REPLACE THEM.

Samuel Anoints David
[1 SAMUEL 16:1-13]

Bible Story Time

Read "Samuel Anoints David" in your *Egermeier's® Bible Story Book*.

Story Background

The story of how the prophet Samuel anointed David to be king is humorous as well as instructive. In Samuel's day, to be anointed meant that oil was poured over a person or object to set it apart as holy to the Lord. For a man, or in this case a boy, to be anointed by the prophet meant that God had chosen him to succeed Israel's first monarch, King Saul.

HOW
DOES GOD
EVALUATE
A PERSON?

READ
1 SAMUEL
16:7.

Jesse had eight sons, and all but the youngest stood before Samuel that day. God had informed Samuel that He had chosen one of Jesse's sons, and some of the sons impressed Samuel, but he didn't feel led by God to anoint any of them. Even though Samuel had been introduced to seven good young men, he had to ask Jesse if he had any more sons. Jesse sent for the youngest one who had been stuck with shepherding duty while the rest of the family was at the party.

When young David, perhaps 10 or 12 years old, walked into the room, Samuel knew he was the one and poured the anointing oil on the boy. Perhaps no one except Samuel and David realized what this anointing was about because life went on as usual for David, and Saul remained king. From that moment, David knew that greatness was expected of him; however, it was a long time before he took the place for which he was chosen.

God has chosen your children as well. Some of them will be leaders; some will be followers. Some may excel in academics, while others will make their living with their hands. The point is that God has a plan for all of them. Wise parents work hard to help each of their children discover that plan. The most difficult aspect of this, though, is when God's plan for them is not the dream the parents have. Sometimes parents have had dreams for themselves that went unfulfilled, and they consciously or unconsciously want to see their kids do what they could not. This can become a point of terrible and long-lasting contention between parent and child. Parents must seek to become their child's biggest encourager, even if God's dream for that child is not the dream the parent would have chosen.

Think & Talk

Ask God to give your child a dream to follow.

What can you say and do that will help your children follow the dream God has for them?

Name some warning signs that would indicate you're pushing the wrong dream on your child. Ask God to give you the wisdom to know when you're doing that.

Fun Times with Younger Kids

Needed: pancakes, fruit cocktail, syrup

Each person will decorate a pancake to look like a face. Use pieces of fruit, chocolate chips, coconut, or nuts to make a nose, mouth, eyes, and even hair on your pancake.

Say: "Anoint" is a new word. In this story Samuel anointed David. That means he poured oil on his head. This was a way for Samuel to show that David was going to do special things for God. We can anoint this pancake; we can pour something on it. How about some syrup!

Each person will experience anointing by pouring syrup on a pancake.

Fun Times with Older Kids

Needed: pennies, 8 empty pop cans

In the first pop can place 1 penny. In the second pop can place

2 pennies. In the third pop can place 3 pennies, and so on until in the eighth pop can you have 8 pennies.

Say: Samuel listened to God, and God told him whom to anoint as the next king. Jesse had 8 sons. Samuel met them, from the oldest down to the youngest, listening for God to tell him which one to anoint.

The 8 pop cans represent the 8 sons of Jesse. Try to put them in order by shaking them. You'll need to listen to the sound and feel the weight of the can.

Say: You couldn't tell what the order should be by looking on the outside of each can. You had to figure out what was inside by listening and testing the weight. Samuel kept looking at the outside appearance of Jesse's sons, but God told Samuel that He was more interested in what was inside—in the heart.

OUR EYES MAY DECEIVE US, BUT GOD NEVER WILL.

David Kills Goliath
[1 SAMUEL 17:1-54]

Bible Story Time *Egermeier's*

Read "David Kills Goliath" in your *Egermeier's® Bible Story Book*.

Story Background

David was still in his teens when the Philistines attacked Israel. His older brothers joined King Saul's army to defend their country, but the war was soon a stalemate as the armies amassed on either side of a valley. Instead of an intense battle at close range, one Philistine giant-of-a-man named Goliath challenged the army of Israel. Goliath proposed that one of Saul's soldiers fight him in single combat instead of a clash of armies. For many days the stalemate continued with Goliath issuing his challenge every morning and evening.

GOLIATH'S HEIGHT WAS 6 CUBITS AND A SPAN, OVER 9 FEET TALL!

One morning, when David's father sent him to take some food to his brothers, David heard the giant's challenge and saw Israel's army shrink in fear. David embarrassed his brothers by saying he could face Goliath. He boldly said he would defeat Goliath and claim the rewards Saul promised. Saul called David to his headquarters and offered the use of his armor. Saul was about 6' 6" tall, and David was not yet full grown. Imagine how comical it must have been when David tried to model Saul's armor! Perhaps he was even laughed out of the king's tent; however, it was no joke to David. He was offended that the Philistine's challenge had gone unanswered. He left the armor behind and chose to fight Goliath the best way he knew.

As a shepherd, David had killed wild beasts that attacked his sheep, and he would use the same tactic with this giant. As David entered the field, Goliath laughed at his young opponent. David, on the other hand, declared that he would defeat Goliath not by his power, but by the power of God. A stone, a sling, a well-aimed throw, and Goliath was down. Suddenly, the shepherd boy was the hero of the nation!

Everyone faces giants of some kind. Some giants are bullies. Some are temptations or bad habits. Some are difficult circumstances. No matter how well you protect your children, they will eventually have to face a giant all alone. David was prepared for Goliath. He had dealt with fear in the field, protecting the sheep. More than that, he was prepared because he was convinced God was with him.

Think & Talk

How are you preparing your children for the giants they may have to face?

GOD WILL HELP US FACE THE GIANTS.

Are you teaching your kids to deal with problems themselves, or do you always step in to solve their conflicts or challenges?

How are you teaching your kids that God is with them and will help them do what is right?

Fun Times with Younger Kids

Needed: ingredients for cookies, waxed paper, kitchen utensils, snack bags

Kids love to be in the kitchen. Help your child make this recipe for Fudge No-Bake Cookies. Bring 2 c. sugar, ½ c. cocoa, ½ c. milk and ½ c. butter to a rolling boil for 2 minutes. Add 3 c. oatmeal, ½ c. peanut butter, a pinch of salt, and ½ t. vanilla. Mix well. Then roll into small bite-size balls and drop onto a piece of waxed paper. (Don't be concerned that they're not all the same size. After all, stones don't all look alike.)

Say: We made some little stones. Who used little stones to do something big? How many stones did David gather from the brook? He gathered 5 stones and put them in his pouch.

Once the no-bake "stones" have cooled, the kids can make snack bags of 5 stones each. Make a list of people the kids can give these little snack bags to and then help deliver them.

Say: King Saul, the army of Israel, and all of David's brothers thought it was impossible for David to take down Goliath. (Isn't it funny, though, that they went ahead and let him try!)

Try to accomplish these tasks. Are they difficult or impossible?

Put a quarter on the floor. Keep your back and heels against the wall and try to pick up the quarter.

Keep your back, heels and shoulders against the wall. Try to jump.

Stand sideways and put your right cheek and your right foot against the wall. Try to lift your left foot.

Bend over and hold the end of your shoes with your hands. Now, try to jump.

Say: Impossible? Oh yeah! These are silly and impossible tasks, but we serve a mighty and powerful God who can make even the impossible possible. What do you think David's brothers thought when they saw David clobber Goliath? David was sure to give God the credit. David couldn't do the impossible, but God could *through* David.

WITH GOD ON YOUR SIDE, ALL THINGS ARE POSSIBLE.

Saul Becomes David's Enemy
[1 SAMUEL 17:55–18:30]

Egermeier's **Bible Story Time**

Read "Saul Becomes David's Enemy" in your *Egermeier's® Bible Story Book*.

Story Background

JEALOUSY CAN QUICKLY TRANSFORM LOVE INTO HATE.

After David defeated Goliath, Saul's army took heart and routed the Philistines. Saul was ecstatic and very proud of the boy hero. He rewarded David by placing him at the head of the army. Everyone was joyful. The women danced and sang in the streets. Saul's celebrating suddenly stopped, though, when he heard the words of a line in their song, *Saul has slain his thousands, and David his tens of thousands* (1 Samuel 18:7, NIV) Joy transformed into jealousy in Saul's heart. He regarded the praise for this new upstart as a personal insult.

Saul was known to have a melancholy (sad) disposition. In fact, on several occasions before his battle with Goliath, David had been called upon to play his lyre for Saul to soothe his depression. Now, Saul could not get the words of the women's song out of his ears. He stewed on them until his admiration for David became raw hate. David continued to make music for Saul, but twice Saul threw his spear at him while he played, causing David to flee for his life. Saul's attitude was so blatantly unfair that Saul's children (Jonathan, who had become David's best friend, and Michal, who would later marry David) protected him from their father and aided his escape.

Even in modern times, some people find it hard to accept the success of others, especially people close to them. This happens a lot with siblings who are competing for their parents' approval. It also happens sometimes when a son or daughter outshines a mom or dad. When children get married, it occurs even more often among in-laws. Parents may not be able to stop this kind of behavior completely, but they can look for ways to restrain it.

How can you and your children avoid the pitfalls of jealousy?

First, look carefully at yourself and guard against envy and jealousy toward a sibling, an in-law, or a child.

Second, do your best to truly rejoice when the people close to you succeed or receive an honor. Wouldn't it be nice to know that your family was in your cheering section? If you want the best for your children, they should be able to depend on your approval for their success without fearing that you will see them as competitors.

Third, try not to pit siblings against each other for your approval. Spread the approval and the cheers around. Let each child have his/her moment.

How are you modeling good relationships—with your siblings, in-laws, and co-workers?

3 STEPS TO AVOID JEALOUSY

Fun Times with Younger Kids

Needed: whipped topping lid, scrap ribbon, crepe paper, paint stir stick, hot glue

Cut the center out of a whipped topping lid (leaving about ¾" around the edge) to make a hoop. Attach 2' lengths of scrap ribbon and crepe paper around the edge with hot glue. Or, you can make a streamer stick by gluing pieces of ribbon and crepe paper to the end of a paint stir stick.

Say: King Saul was jealous of David because the women were singing and dancing to celebrate David's victories. They probably would've danced with hoops and sticks something like these as they went through the streets.

Make up a simple song about David to a familiar tune. Then use the hoops and streamer sticks to dance along with the song.

Needed: baking soda, vinegar, small cup, pie pan

Say: King Saul didn't like that the people were singing about how wonderful David was. It made the king insecure, thinking that the people liked David more than they liked him. He wasn't sure where he stood with the people.

Set the cup in the pie pan. Put ¼ cup of baking soda in the cup.

Say: This baking soda is insecurity—not knowing where you stand. King Saul wanted the singing to be about him...not David. He was jealous of all the attention David was getting. This vinegar is going to represent jealousy. What happens when we mix baking soda and vinegar together?

Pour some vinegar slowly into the baking soda and watch what happens.

Say: What happens when we mix insecurity and jealousy? You get anger! That's what happened to King Saul. He was insecure and jealous...and then he really got angry at David. Who have you been jealous of? Have you ever found yourself getting angry with someone just because they could do something better than you could?

DON'T LET YOUR JEALOUSY BOIL OVER!

Jonathan Warns David

[1 SAMUEL 20]

Bible Story Time *Egermeier's*

Read "Jonathan Warns David" in your *Egermeier's® Bible Story Book*.

Story Background

Saul's hatred of David seemed to come and go. Sometimes he was glad to have David and his lyre close by, and sometimes his anger reached a lethal level. Jonathan was convinced, or perhaps he hoped, Saul's anger had subsided, but David wasn't as sure. Together, they came up with a way to discover the truth. They worked the plan and discovered Saul's anger burned hot, so hot that he tried to kill Jonathan when he verbally defended David. In his anger, Saul said something that would turn out to be true—that as long as David was alive, Jonathan would never be king. Whether or not Jonathan realized the truth of that statement, we don't know, but we do know Jonathan's devotion to David was very deep. He loved David and could see God's hand on him.

A LYRE IS A MUSICAL INSTRUMENT SIMILAR IN APPEARANCE TO A SMALL HARP.

At the risk of alienating the father he loved and losing his chance to rule the kingdom, Jonathan proved to be a true friend to David. Many people are friends...until their friendship costs them something. Jonathan's friendship with David had the potential to cost Jonathan *everything*; however, Jonathan knew for certain that without his help David would die. He came through for David, and David never forgot that unselfish love. Jonathan was killed in battle before David could repay him personally, but later in life, he took care of Jonathan's crippled son, Mephibosheth.

The love Jonathan had for his friend, David, is an example of the kind of love Jesus taught. This love reveals itself in the desire to help the loved one. This kind of love does not depend on being returned. It says, "I love you." Period. End of sentence. Other kinds of love say, "I love you, but..." or "I love you when..." or "I love you until..." or "I love you unless..." or "I love you as long as…." Jonathan's brand of selfless love is the kind Jesus wants His followers to have for one another. It's love that lasts. Jonathan and David were men's men, who shared this kind of deep friendship.

This love is important for families too. While it may not be the kind of love that attracts married couples to each other, it is the kind of love that makes 50th wedding anniversaries. It's the deeply devoted love couples vow to share on their wedding day, and it's the way children should experience their parents' love for them. Imagine how great family life would be if siblings cared for each other without reservation.

Think & Talk

When have you added *but, when, until, unless,* or *as long as,* either out loud or mentally, after saying, "I love you"? When have you added any of those words after agreeing to do something for your spouse or children?

Think of a friend you have had for a lifetime. How far does your friendship go?

How can you help your child cultivate strong, lifetime friendships?

HUMANS LOVE CONDITIONALLY; GOD LOVES UNCONDITIONALLY.

Fun Times with Younger Kids

Needed: drinking straws, pennies, tape, paper plate

Say: Jonathan must have been really good with his bow and arrows. He knew exactly how far the arrows would go and where they would land. Jonathan and David were best friends and looked out for each other. They used the arrow to signal whether or not David was safe from King Saul.

Put the end of a straw between 2 pennies and wrap them with tape, so the pennies are secure on the end of the straw. Make several of these to be the arrows in the game. Lay a paper plate on the floor. (If you have a hula hoop, color the paper plate red and lay it in the center of the hoop as the bulls-eye of the target.) Determine a stand-behind line for different ages. Toss the straws at the paper plate to see if you can hit the mark—the bulls-eye of the target.

Needed: pairs of socks, bucket

Say: How would David know that Saul was after him and that he should get away? Jonathan would shoot his arrow BEYOND the rock where David was. Jonathan must've been really good with a bow and arrow!

Roll some socks into themselves to make soft balls. Place a bucket behind a chair, preferably an upholstered chair. Stand about 6 feet in front of the chair. Take turns tossing the sock balls over the chair to see if you can get them to land in the bucket. Each time one goes in, the tosser must say, "Run, David, run!"

David Finds Saul Asleep
[1 SAMUEL 26–27]

Egermeier's Bible Story Time

Read "David Finds Saul Asleep" in your *Egermeier's® Bible Story Book.*

Story Background

When David found Saul asleep, he had his second opportunity to kill Saul. David would have been justified in taking Saul's life either time. Both times Saul led an army to hunt down and kill David and his men. Each time, David chose not to get revenge, but to save himself from Saul's relentless pursuit. When David's men urged him to kill Saul, David said he would never lift his hand against the Lord's anointed. He remained faithful to the idea that God made Saul king and that he should remain king until God removed him.

READ WHAT
JESUS SAID
ABOUT
REVENGE IN
MATTHEW
5:38-42.

We learn a lot about David's character here. He had the ability to forbear. "Forbear" is a word seldom seen outside the Bible, but it's a very important term for civilization. To forbear is to refrain from revenge even when that revenge may be justified or justifiable. Did you get that? To forbear is to refrain from revenge even when that revenge may be justified or justifiable. Later Jesus would teach a now famous lesson on forbearance. Remember, "Turn the other cheek"?

David spared Saul even though David knew God planned for him to one day be king. He could have sped up the process by killing Saul and taking the throne.

However, if David had killed Saul, a blood feud may have begun that would always have plagued Israel. David chose another course.

Many family problems, and even problems between nations and ethnic groups, continue because no one is willing to forbear. David's physical courage was unquestioned, and by choosing not to kill Saul when he had the chance, he showed his courage went deeper. David set an example that real men don't always have to get even.

Think & Talk

Who has hurt or offended you? Did you feel the need to get back at them? What form did that take?

Is there someone who deserves your anger? Do you have the courage to forbear? How do you go about doing that?

How are you teaching your children forbearance? By word? By your actions?

Are your kids learning that real courage goes deeper than physical courage?

Fun Times with Younger Kids

Needed: blindfold, water bottle

Say: David found Saul asleep with his spear and water bottle close by him. David took the spear and water bottle to prove to King Saul that he could have harmed him while he slept.

Start off by blindfolding a parent. The adult will lay on his/her side on the floor with a water bottle within arm's reach. Another family member will try to quietly sneak up on the blindfolded parent and grab the water bottle without being caught. The blindfolded parent will try to tag whoever is grabbing the bottle. After the kids get the idea of what you are doing, blindfold them so they can try to tag anyone attempting to take the bottle.

Fun Times with Older Kids

Needed: piece of cardboard

Cut a piece of scrap cardboard to make a 3" or 4" square. Two members of the family will face each other, so that you are nose-to-nose. (Adults may have to get on their knees.) Place the piece of cardboard between your noses, then try to walk to the other end of the room without dropping the cardboard.

Read what Jesus said about loving our enemies in Matthew 5:43-47.

Say: Was this easy, difficult, or super duper difficult? Sometimes God asks you to do difficult things, really difficult things…not carrying cardboard between your noses, but things like loving your enemies. He says that if you're really following Him, you have to love everyone—the bullies at school, the lazy workers who take advantage of you on the job, people who try to do our country harm. Who else does God tell you to love? How difficult do you think it was for David to keep from hurting King Saul? In spite of what the king was doing to David, David had to respect, honor, and love him. David did it with God's help, and you can love your enemies also…but only with God's help.

The Lame Prince
(2 SAMUEL 4:4; 9:1-13)

Read "The Lame Prince" in your *Egermeier's® Bible Story Book.*

Story Background

A battle with the Philistines took the lives of Saul and Jonathan and finally ended the reign of Israel's first king. In the tremendous panic that followed, one of Jonathan's servants picked up his 5-year-old son, Prince Mephibosheth, to escape the oncoming Philistine army. In her hurry she stumbled and dropped the prince and, perhaps, fell on him. The result was that Mephibosheth's feet were permanently crippled. The prince escaped and was taken in and cared for on the other side of the Jordan River.

David always mourned Saul and especially his good friend, Jonathan. Years later, after he became king and subdued the Philistines, David ordered a search to see if any of Jonathan's family had survived the war. Mephibosheth was found and brought to David's palace. Mephibosheth must have been frightened when he was summoned to the presence of the king whom he had not met, but David was overjoyed at finding the son of his best friend. David made him part of his court and restored Saul's lands to him.

Again, we see David as the "man after God's heart." Most rulers would have exterminated the last of Saul's heirs to eliminate permanently any claim to the throne from that family. David chose another way. He chose charity, which is the highest form of love. Charity gives without expecting anything in return. Mephibosheth had nothing to offer David. While he represented a link to Jonathan, he wouldn't even have had many memories to share with David of his father, who died when he was so young. By providing for Mephibosheth, David honored the memory of Jonathan, yet he could have built a statue for that. Instead, he gave to this crippled man, expecting to receive nothing from him.

CHARITY GIVES, EXPECTING NOTHING IN RETURN.

Take a moment to read 1 Corinthians 13 in your Bible. This passage illustrates the kind of love Christ-followers should share with others. The King James Version uses the word "charity," while more modern translations use the word "love" for the Greek word "agape." David's care for Mephibosheth is this kind of love.

Think & Talk

How are you teaching charity in your family?

Do your children give to and do things for people who can never repay them? When have you given them the opportunity to be charitable?

How are you teaching your children to do things for each other without insisting on payback?

Fun Times with Younger Kids

Needed: Pez® dispenser

Say: King David was very kind to Mephibosheth, and he didn't have to be. We have the chance every day to be kind to others, even when we don't have to be, even when we're not told to be kind.

Think of kind things you could say or kind things you could do. Each time someone offers a suggestion about how to be kind in everyday life, let that person squeeze the Pez® dispenser and take one little candy. Now, actually do these things. Repeat the Pez® dispensing each time the kindness is done or said.

Fun Times with Older Kids

Say: King David was kind to Mephibosheth when he didn't have to be. He could've just let things stay the way they were and not tried to find Jonathan's son. But he chose to be kind, and that's why we know about this story; otherwise, we may never have known the name Mephibosheth.

Make a list of random acts of kindness you could do.

Say: What is a random act of kindness anyway? It's when you do something kind when it's not expected.

Decide which things on your list you are going to do.

Say: When you put your kindness into action, you'll see a change in the people around you, but more than that, you'll see a change in yourself.

Here are a few ideas to get you started.

Help someone put their bags of groceries in their car and then return their cart for them.

Make a casserole for someone who is homebound or just in a very busy time in his/her life.

Use a hand vacuum cleaner to clean out the car…or your sofa.

Let someone go in front of you in the checkout line.

Put together a care package of kids' activities that you could donate to a local children's hospital.

HOW MANY MORE RANDOM ACTS OF KINDNESS CAN YOU THINK OF?

God Gives Solomon a Gift
[1 KINGS 3–4]

Read "God Gives Solomon a Gift" in your *Egermeier's*® *Bible Story Book*.

Story Background

Geographically, the land of Israel has always been a strategic place. It is a crossroads where three continents—Asia, Europe, and Africa—meet. In ancient times, it sat between great empires: Egypt to the south; (at various times in history) Sumer, Babylon, Assyria, and Persia to the east; and the Hittites, Greece and Rome to the north. The empires fought on, over, and through the land God had promised to His people. Most of the time, Israel was at war with or under the thumb of one of them. During the time of kings Saul, David, and Solomon, however, the great empires withdrew, and Israel enjoyed its golden age.

ISRAEL WAS THE CROSSROADS FOR RELIGIOUS LEARNING.

Israel's land and population were small, yet it was a great place for the transfer of religious thought because so many people from other lands and schools of thought passed through it. In other words, God chose for His people to live in the middle of the world's equivalent to the intersection of Broadway and Main Street in Anytown, USA. Because of this, life was often hard for God's people, but they were also in a great place to send God's message to all parts of the globe.

The days of David and Solomon were the glory days for Israel in many ways. The kingdom reached its peak in size, riches, and power. This period was the only time during the Old Testament that the people lived in the Promised Land in unity. Solomon, David's son and successor, was a great king. Soon after taking the throne, Solomon asked God to bless him with wisdom instead of asking for wealth and power. God chose to give him all three, and Solomon's name has now become synonymous with wisdom. Though he ruled wisely in many ways, the rest of the world influenced Solomon and his kingdom. (This is one of the dangers of living in a busy intersection.) Solomon took many wives from places that worshiped various gods. The consequence of this would be chaos in the years following Solomon's reign.

The lesson of Solomon is to do what is necessary to stay humble, and renew your commitment to do what God commands. Solomon started out well; unfortunately, he got off track and was distracted as the years went by.

Think & Talk

How do you keep your relationship with Jesus fresh?

Who helps you see when you are getting off track?

How are you guarding your priorities?

Fun Times with Younger Kids

Needed: bucket of sand, quarters, slotted spoon

Mix some quarters into a bucket of sand. Then each person will have 10 seconds (everyone count out loud) to use the spoon in the sand to find quarters. You are "mining" for quarters.

Say: When you look for gold in rock, that's called "mining." When you search for coal down in the ground, that's called "mining." "Mining" is when you are looking for something precious, something important to you, something more valuable than other things. We have to look for it to be able to find it.

If your kids have seen the movie "Aladdin," **say:** What happened when Aladdin's lamp was rubbed? The genie came out and offered to grant three wishes. God isn't in a magic lamp, but He did ask Solomon what he wished for more than anything else. Solomon didn't say that he wanted to be rich or handsome. He wanted wisdom. He was searching for… mining…wisdom, and God gave him great wisdom to rule the people. We can be wise too by listening to God, looking for His answers, and doing what we know God wants us to do.

Fun Times with Older Kids

HOW CAN
WE BECOME
WISE LIKE
SOLOMON?

READ
JAMES 1:5.

Play a fun game of "20 Questions" with the names of animals. One person will think of an animal. Then everyone else takes turns asking questions that can be answered "yes" or "no." When a player thinks he/she knows what the animal is, guess it on the next turn.

Say: What does this game have to do with being wise like Solomon? Being wise isn't just being smart. It's figuring out the right thing to do, and then actually doing it. But how do we know what is the right thing—the wise thing—to do? One main way is by asking questions. Who should you ask questions of? Ask people you trust. Ask God when you pray. Go to the Bible with your questions, and it will give you guidelines for making wise choices.

Elijah Is Fed by Ravens
[1 KINGS 16:29–17:9]

Bible Story Time *Egermeier's*

Read "Elijah Is Fed by Ravens" in your *Egermeier's*® *Bible Story Book.*

Story Background

In the years after the reign of Solomon, Israel was wracked by civil war and was finally divided into two kingdoms: Israel and Judah. The leadership in Israel, which was the new northern kingdom, passed from bad king to bad king to Ahab. Rulers couldn't get much worse than Ahab and his horrible bride, Jezebel. These two turned Israel, home to the people of God, into a place where the worship of fertility gods was more than tolerated. Baal worship had become the "in" thing for all the fine folks of Israel. There were altars to Baal and poles for his consort goddess, Asherah, on every hill (called high places) in the country.

Into this pagan, corrupt mess walked Elijah, the man God chose to use at this point in history. He pronounced this simple prophecy to Ahab: it will not rain until further notice. How this rough-hewn man, dressed in camel hair (not the same as a camel hair sport coat), got close to King Ahab is a mystery. He was so out of place and such an oddity in the court of Ahab that he and his prophecy were simply ignored as the ravings of some kind of religious nut. This continued until it became obvious that a severe drought had struck. That's when Ahab began a full-scale search for the strange man who claimed to speak for God.

All this time Elijah had been way off the beaten path, camping by a brook. He ate food that God sent to him by ravens, and he had all the water he needed until the brook dried up. Then God sent him to Zaraphath where He made provision for Elijah to be fed by a poor widow.

The lesson for us is that God takes care of us when we do His

TO MAKE JEZEBEL HAPPY, AHAB EVEN BUILT A TEMPLE AND ALTAR FOR BAAL WORSHIP.

will. Elijah's accommodations were not what he would have received at a Ritz-Carlton, but God provided for him. We can rest assured this same God will make provision for us when we persist in being who He wants us to be in the face of opposition.

Think & Talk

Are you in the center of God's will for your life? How do you sense that?

What circumstance or person in your life makes it particularly hard to live by Christian principles?

When are you aware that you need more faith to trust in God's ability to provide for you? How can following Him more completely take the stress out of those times?

Fun Times with Younger Kids

Needed: piece of bread, feather boa (optional)

Say: God sent the ravens to deliver food to Elijah. How did the birds get the food to Elijah? They flew with it around and over all kinds of things! What do you think they had to go around? What do you think they had to fly over?

GOD USED RAVENS TO PROVIDE FOR ELIJAH. HAS GOD EVER PROVIDED FOR YOU IN AN UNUSUAL WAY?

If you have a feather boa, then drape it over your preschooler's shoulders, so they can grab hold of each end in their hands. They will hold a piece of bread in their teeth as they follow your instructions about where to fly.

Fly around the kitchen island.

Fly under the dining room table.

Fly over the footstool in the living room.

Fly through a hula hoop.

Fly over your bed.

Fly into the bathtub and out again.

Needed: drinking straw, scissors, soft snacks

Gather some soft snacks that your kids will enjoy: hot dogs, marshmallows, bread, and all kinds of fruit. Cut a straw in three equal sections.

Say: Elijah was hiding from King Ahab and was on the run, hanging out by a brook. Because Elijah was so far away from home or a town, God sent ravens to feed Elijah. What food did the ravens carry to Elijah? We're going to pretend to be the ravens and feed one another our snacks.

One person will take a piece of the straw and ask one of the other family members what they would like to eat. They will hold the straw between their teeth and stick the other end of the straw into the food that was requested. Then, they will pretend to fly to that person to deliver the food. Remember to make bird sounds and flap your wings! Gently place the end of the straw with the food on it in the person's mouth and let them pull it off. Yum! Keep feeding each other in this way until you all have your fill. (Rinse straws between uses, or make sure the straw goes to the same person each time.)

Elijah and the Prophets of Baal
[1 KINGS 18:17-40]

Egermeier's Bible Story Time

Read "Elijah and the Prophets of Baal" in your *Egermeier's®
Bible Story Book.*

Story Background

MT. CARMEL IS
A MOUNTAIN
RANGE IN
NORTHEASTERN
ISRAEL NEAR THE
MEDITERRANEAN
SEA.

This story is like an Old West showdown. Elijah stands alone
on Mt. Carmel, facing 450 prophets of Baal. Actually, it was not
really a fair fight because Elijah had a tremendous advantage—
God was on his side. The prophets of Baal only had their
false fertility god represented by idols. Elijah had the creator
God who is beyond being contained in a statue or a building.
(There was a temple in Jerusalem, but no one thought God was
contained in it.) Realizing his advantage, Elijah invited the Baal
boys to go first. The object was for them to build an altar, lay a
sacrifice on it for Baal, and then Elijah would do the same for
Yahweh, God. The deity that responded by igniting the sacrifice
would be known as the true God, once and for all. After Baal's
prophets laid the sacrifice, they called to him. They danced…
they hollered…they chanted…and they even cut themselves to
show Baal their sincerity, but their altar remained cold. Elijah
couldn't resist getting in a few jeers at their expense.

When it was Elijah's turn, he must have been embarrassed for
the pagan prophets because he created an additional challenge
for Yahweh. He covered the sacrifice, the wood, and the altar
with gallons and gallons of water. Then he offered a very simple
prayer, asking God to show Himself so that the people might
know what Elijah already knew—Yahweh is God, the only
God. Fire fell! In response, the people promptly rose up and
killed all the prophets of Baal.

Elijah didn't need to coax God because he was in the center
of God's will that day. Baal worship was popular and favored
by Queen Jezebel. Baal was the fad of the day. But Elijah knew
his God was no fad. He knew God had blessed him and had a
history of blessing His people.

Many times you and your children will be in situations where the idea of serving God is foreign to the "in" group. Sometimes, being a Christ-follower puts you in the minority. At times you may even find yourself ridiculed for your lifestyle and beliefs. Your faith must be rooted deeply so that it can stand in those times. When you spend time with your kids, focusing on the Bible, you are taking a step toward growing deep roots. Parents, make sure your everyday life, your attitudes, your priorities, and your choices are teaching your children the presence and power of God.

A DEEP FAITH IN GOD HELPS US WITHSTAND LIFE'S STORMS.

Think & Talk

What challenges to their faith are your children facing now? Do they talk to you about those challenges?

Listening is important. Hear your children out before you give them advice or answers to their problems. Avoid easy "Sunday school" answers.

Help your kids know they are not the only ones who deal with challenges to their faith. Assure them that God will help them. You can affirm that by sharing your experiences with them.

Fun Times with Younger Kids

Needed: aluminum foil, cookie sheet, cheese grater, old red, yellow, and orange crayons

Wad up 12 pieces of aluminum foil to represent the 12 stones that Elijah used for the altar. Place these on a foil-lined cookie sheet. Preheat the oven to 400 degrees. Then pull the paper off of old crayons—red, yellow, and orange. Show your kids how to rub the end of the crayon against the grater to make shavings, and when to stop so their fingers don't get too close to the grater. Sprinkle the shavings over the 12 foil stones and place the cookie sheet in the oven for 5 minutes, or until the crayons have melted.

Say: Whose sacrifice burned up—Baal's prophets' or Elijah's? Who was God pleased with?

STAND UP FOR THE TRUTH!

Needed: candle, matches

You may have done this very simple science experiment as a child. Light a candle and let it burn for a minute. Blow it out and watch the trail of smoke. Light a match and hold it in the trail of smoke, moving it closer to the candle. It will reignite the candle without touching the wick!

Say: This seems like a very strange way to light a candle. Describe the strange way that God lit the altar in this story. There were lots of people who believed that a made-up god, Baal, could ignite the altar. Just because lots of people thought it was so, didn't make it the truth. Elijah worshipped God even though it seemed that he was the only one who did. Elijah was right, and God proved Himself. When you have the truth on your side, sometime you may have to stand alone too.

Elijah and the Still Small Voice
[1 KINGS 19:9-21]

Bible Story Time *Egermeier's*

Read "Elijah and the Still Small Voice" in your *Egermeier's®
Bible Story Book*.

Story Background

After the victory over the prophets of Baal, Elijah prayed and
the rains came. Still Ahab and Jezebel resisted God and made
Elijah a wanted man. Once again, Elijah was in hiding—this
time in a cave in the mountain where Moses received the Ten
Commandments long before. Elijah was in a deep depression.
He had gone from the tremendous high when the fire fell and
the rains came, to the awful low of being hunted like an animal.
God came to this wreck of a man and simply asked him, "What
are you doing here?" Elijah's answer revealed his depression.

It almost sounded like, "Nobody likes me. Everybody hates me.
I'm gonna eat some worms." That's when God demonstrated
that He is not always found in the spectacular (the big wind,
the earthquake, the fire), but sometimes God is in the "still
small voice." Elijah didn't quite get it yet because when the still
small voice asked him the same question, Elijah gave the same
answer, full of self-pity. God did three things that pulled Elijah
out of his depression: 1) He told him he was not the only one
who was listening to God. 2) He gave him something to do. 3)
He gave him Elisha to teach and invest his life in.

Depression is a major problem for many in our society. Difficult
circumstances can bring us down, and ironically sometimes
we, who have so much, get hung up on what we don't have.
Often people turn to a doctor for help; perhaps, we should
consider turning to God. We may just hear the still small voice
reminding us that we are not alone and that God is giving us
an assignment. Parents, you have a built-in assignment. You
have little Elishas in your home who need you to teach them
with your life and love, as well as your words. No matter what

GOD SPEAKS
WHEN WE
QUIET OUR
HEARTS AND
LISTEN.

your circumstances are, take heart and remember that you are someone very special and have this wonderful assignment to do.

Think & Talk

When do you feel most alone? Write down some practical things you can do when those times come. Tuck the notes away where you'll run across them often.

What is the best way for you to quiet yourself so you can hear the still small voice of God?

Fun Times with Younger Kids

Needed: timer

Set a timer for one minute and challenge your kids to remain completely quiet for the entire minute. While they are being quiet, encourage them to think about the little noises they can hear. One minute seems like a very quick amount of time, but when you're being very still—and when you're a preschooler— it can feel like an eternity!

Say: What did you hear? Would you have heard those noises if you were being loud and crazy? Do you sometimes not hear when your mommy is calling because you are being too noisy or the TV is up too loud? God wants us to be quiet for a while and think about Him.

Make a statement in a whisper and see if your children can understand what you are saying. They have to be very quiet to hear you. Then trade roles and see if you can hear their whispers.

Fun Times with Older Kids

Needed: kitchen utensils

Take everyone into the kitchen and tell them that you're going to read 1 Kings 19:9-21 to them there. Before you start reading, though, create a lot of noise by turning on some music and appliances—dishwasher, blender, mixer, food grinder, etc. Give everyone a utensil to beat against a pan. Begin reading in a normal voice. As you read, take a utensil away from one person, then another, and turn off appliances one by one until the room is quiet again.

Say: Why was it difficult for you to understand what I was saying when I first began reading? When did it get easier? How is this like understanding God? How should we prepare our hearts and environments when we're studying His Word? God doesn't ask you to be silent all the time, but He wants you to quiet your mind and heart so He can teach and help you.

A SCRIPTURE TO MEMORIZE:
BE STILL, AND KNOW THAT I AM GOD.
PSALM 46:10

A Little Slave Girl Helps Naaman
[2 KINGS 5:1–14]

Egermeier's **Bible Story Time**

Read "A Little Slave Girl Helps Naaman" in your *Egermeier's® Bible Story Book*.

Story Background

In Bible times leprosy was usually incurable. Today it is curable, although leper colonies can still be found in countries where medical care is poor.

There are three points to contemplate in this story. First, the child's simple faith was eloquent. The little girl didn't know much about the religious differences between the cultures of Israel and Syria. She simply believed God used the prophet Elisha. She didn't understand that submitting to a prophet in Israel might be politically uncomfortable for a captain in Syria's army, nor that it would be hard socially for a man like Naaman to put himself in the hands of a God he knew very little about. But the girl's faith spoke hope into Naaman's life, and hope trumps just about everything else.

Second, Naaman had to humble himself to do what Elisha ordered. Naaman was used to giving orders; now he had to carry out what seemed to be a very illogical order—to bathe in the muddy Jordan River. The lesson is that God's tools and His methods are often surprising. Bathing in dirty water does not seem like a good way to cleanse yourself and cure a skin disease.

Third, once Naaman chose to do things Elisha's way, he had to be persistent. It took dipping his body seven times in the Jordan for the healing to take place. Oftentimes, God calls on us to be persistent in our prayers, in our priorities, and in our love. The blessing Naaman sought came, but he was required to be patient and obedient to receive it.

Think & Talk

How do you sometimes complicate your faith? Do you need to simply believe God?

In what area in your life might you be too proud to do what

needs to be done to reach a goal or receive a blessing?

Have you given up too soon? Is there something you should try again?

Fun Times with Younger Kids

Say: Most of the time, we get the job done when we do it ONCE. But how many times did Naaman have to dip himself in the Jordan River? Seven times! Once was not enough. What would happen if you were told to do something again… and again…and again…and again…and again…and again? You'd probably whine and complain.

Do some of these things with your child 7 times, and count out loud as you do.

Dip a cookie 7 times in a glass of chocolate milk.

Squirt your child with foam soap (or shaving cream) in the bathtub and then have him/her dip themselves 7 times to remove it.

Dip a piece of bread 7 times in some soup.

Fill the kitchen sink with water and dip a doll in the water 7 times.

Fun Times with Older Kids

Needed: treat, ball cap, tea bag, packing tape

With a piece of packing tape, attach a tea bag label to the ball cap, so the bag hangs down over the edge of the bill. One person will wear the hat. (Make sure it fits snuggly.) At your signal, the person will try to swing the tea bag so that it rests on the bill. Let them know beforehand that when they complete that task you have a treat for them.

Say: You were just asked to do something rather strange in order to get a treat. It wasn't easy, was it? Who in this story was asked to do something strange? Naaman was asked to dip in the muddy Jordan River seven times, but the little slave girl had to do something unusual also. She had to love the man, who really was her enemy, enough to help him be healed. Name someone who is difficult for you to love. What can you do to step out and show him/her love?

Food for a Starving City
[2 KINGS 6:24—7:20]

Egermeier's Bible Story Time

Read "Food for a Starving City" in your *Egermeier's® Bible Story Book.*

Story Background

Leprosy was a much-dreaded disease in Israel during Bible times, and it still is today in some places. This terrible, progressive infection attacks and deforms the skin. Eventually, it renders the sufferer unable to fight off other infections. As leprosy progresses, its effects become horrific, and the infected person becomes very difficult to look at, even for himself. In Bible times and even today, victims of this disease have been segregated from the rest of society into asylums or colonies. People have always feared the disease, and those who were afflicted with it. In Jesus' time lepers were required to shout "Unclean!" to warn uninfected people of their presence.

In this story, four such unfortunates play a prominent role. They were on the outside of a starving, besieged city. The last thing the citizens of Samaria needed was an outbreak of leprosy, so the lepers were caught between the walls of a city under attack and the attacking army. After weighing their options they decided to surrender to the attacking Syrians in hopes that they might be given food and left alone because of their illness. When they entered the Syrian camp, though, they found it deserted. The army had vanished and left everything behind! The four lepers first ate their fill, and then they began hoarding all the best items they could find. They were suddenly rich! The starving people in Samaria were unaware that the Syrians had left and the siege was broken. Everything in the camp belonged to these four lepers.

Before long, however, the lepers realized two things. They could do nothing with their gains because they still had leprosy, and because of the leprosy they would still be ostracized from society. Secondly, the people in the town were starving and

JESUS HEALED LEPERS AND TOUCHED THE UNTOUCHABLE. READ MATTHEW 8:1-4 AND LUKE 17:11-19.

needed the things the four were now enjoying. These four terminally ill men did a gracious thing. They went to the city gates and told the news. At first they were not believed, but soon someone was sent to investigate, and the result was that Samaria was saved.

The four lepers could have walked away with all they could carry. It might have been a few days before the Samarians realized the Syrians were gone, and some Samarians probably would have starved in the meantime. Instead, the four lepers exercised grace. They gave grace to the people who had shunned them and put them out, and sadly we don't have any record of the four being thanked. Their grace went beyond thought of thanks or reward. They did the right thing because it was the right thing.

Sometimes, we have to take our own interests out of the equation and just do what is right because it's right.

GOD GIVES US GRACE BY HELPING US WHEN WE DON'T DESERVE IT.

Think & Talk

When have you offered grace? In what instance do you regret passing up the opportunity to do what was right for no other reason except that it was the right thing to do?

How can you teach your children this kind of grace and attitude?

Fun Times with Younger Kids

Say: When the four men in the story discovered a source of food for the starving city, they shared it with them. There are people in our town who are hungry and may not have any food in their cabinets for their next meal. You can be the one who helps them get their next meal.

Choose one food that you will collect as a family. (Soup is an excellent item to collect because almost everyone has a can in their cupboard.) Decide on different ways that you can collect your food item this next week. Go through your cabinets for appropriate cans. You may walk through your neighborhood with a wagon to ask neighbors to contribute. Let your child help you make a poster you can put on your desk at work. Ask the church office if you can put a box for collecting cans at one of the entrances. Take your child with you when you deliver the cans to an organization that will distribute them.

Fun Times with Older Kids

Say: Even though the Samarians were fighting against the Syrians, their main problem was that they were starving to death! There are people this very day who are starving to death—people who live in your community, in a different state, or on the other side of the world. They are probably people you don't know or may be people you don't like, but that shouldn't matter. They have a need and you have a way to help! Feeding them is one way to show grace and do the right thing, just because it's the right thing to do.

This is a great exercise for your child on so many different levels. Take your child to a grocery store and give him/her a certain amount of money. Create a make-believe family and with this amount of money, try to feed them. You may need to guide your child in how far certain foods will stretch, how they need to be stored (because the family this food will be given to may not have refrigeration), and the difficulty of preparation. Then package the groceries and take them to a facility where they can be distributed.

SOME STATISTICS INDICATE 1 IN 6 PEOPLE IN THE U.S. GO HUNGRY. IMAGINE WHAT THE STATISTICS ARE IN THIRD WORLD COUNTRIES. USE YOUR COMPUTER OR A LIBRARY TO FIND OUT.

Jonah Disobeys God
[JONAH 1–2]

Bible Story Time *Egermeier's*

Read "Jonah Disobeys God" in your *Egermeier's® Bible Story Book*.

Story Background

Some people have to learn the hard way, and Jonah was one of those people. The lesson he had to learn was actually pretty simple: you can't run away from God. If you believe God is everywhere, knows everything, and is all-powerful, then the idea of running from Him can be nothing but dumb. Yet Jonah tried to run from what God wanted him to do. Maybe he thought he knew better than God what should be done with the Ninevites, or perhaps he hated them and didn't want them to find God's forgiveness. Maybe he thought they would never be interested in God. He could have feared them so much that he just ran. Whatever the reason, the outcome was that God told him to leave Israel and go east to Nineveh to preach to the Assyrians, and Jonah chose to go west to the opposite end of the known world.

God chose a very novel approach for getting Jonah to do the task he had given him. Three days inside a big fish (or a whale) would be an unpleasant experience for anyone, but it literally put the fear of God into Jonah. Finally, he picked himself up and did as he was told.

OMNIPRESENT: GOD IS EVERYWHERE. OMNISCIENT: GOD KNOWS EVERYTHING. OMNIPOTENT: GOD IS ALL-POWERFUL.

Think & Talk

Don't try to run from God. He has ways you have never even thought of to get your attention!

Don't let anyone or anything scare you from doing God's work. God's methods of correction can be scarier.

Don't let your prejudice about people keep you from sharing God's love with them. Don't assume the roughest, toughest people can't be touched by God.

Finally, try not to get swallowed by a big fish. It must have taken Jonah days to get the gunk and stink off!

Fun Times with Younger Kids

Needed: gallon milk jug, box cutter, black permanent marker, plastic person (Legos®)

Using a boxcutter, cut the bottom out of a plastic milk jug and outline the edges with a black permanent marker. Draw eyes on the side to make a big fish. Now, have some fun in the bathtub! Place a plastic toy person or one made from Legos® in the water. Use the fish milk jug to scoop up the person, and encourage your child to say, "A big fish swallowed Jonah!" Then when the child dumps the plastic person out, say, "Jonah is going to obey God now."

Say: When is it hard for you to obey Mommy or Daddy? Why don't you want to obey sometimes? How does it make your parents feel when you don't obey them? How do you think God felt when Jonah didn't do what He told him to do?

Fun Times for Older Kids

Needed: drinking straws, M&Ms®, paper, pencil

Say: Jonah was in several different places during this story. Let's name them. He started out at his home around Joppa. Then he boarded a ship. He was thrown overboard and spent 3 days in a big fish. The fish spit him out onto the shore. Then he went to Nineveh.

Write each place on a separate piece of paper: Home, Ship, Fish, Shore, Nineveh. Place these papers around your house. Assign a color of M&M® to each family member and put those colors on each paper. Now, give each family member a drinking straw. At the signal, everyone will go to the paper labeled "Home" and pick up his/her color of M&M® by sucking it up to the end of the straw. Then transport the M&M® to the next paper, "Ship," without letting it fall off the end of the straw. There, release that M&M® and eat it. Now, pick up the next M&M® and transport it in the same fashion to the "Fish." Continue doing this until you've been all 5 places that Jonah was…and eaten all 5 M&Ms®!

Israel Is Enslaved

(2 KINGS 17)

Read "Israel Is Enslaved" in your *Egermeier's® Bible Story Book*.

Bible Story Time *Egermeier's*

Story Background

Through the preaching of Jonah, Assyria repented and for many years Israel was safe. As the Assyrians continued to rise in power and influence, however, they eventually were ready to take Israel. In the meantime, Israel had turned its back on God again and again. Finally, God removed His protection, and Assyria not only invaded Israel, but also moved nearly all the people to another part of the vast empire. Then Assyria repopulated the land with conquered people from other places.

Ten of the tribes of Jacob's family were lost to history; no one is sure what happened to them. Some of their descendants may have filtered back to the area from time to time, but generally those ten tribes of the northern kingdom of Israel are known as "the lost tribes." The southern kingdom of Judah remained. It was established when Israel was divided in the chaos that followed after Solomon died. Judah was home to two of the original twelve tribes: Judah and Benjamin. Israel had always been the wealthier and more sophisticated kingdom, with better land and more cities. Judah, however, had Jerusalem and the temple Solomon had built. Both kingdoms were infected by other religions, but Israel seemed to be more susceptible to the fertility cult of Baal. Judah continued to exist after Israel's fall by paying tribute to the Assyrians.

The story of the fall and disappearance of the kingdom of Israel is a cautionary tale to us. God loved Israel. God had given Israel its very existence. God simply wanted to be their God and for them to be His people. He sent prophet after prophet to warn and bring them back to Him, but in the end, the time came and He let Israel fall.

God loves us and wants the best for us. He simply wants to be

TRIBUTE WAS A PAYMENT FROM ONE NATION TO ANOTHER TO SHOW SUBMISSION OR TO ENSURE PROTECTION.

our God and for us to be His people. God patiently waits for us to return His love and participate in a close relationship with Him. He is disappointed when we stray, and He is hurt when we deny Him, but God is willing to do everything possible to be close to us. God proved that by sending His Son to live, die, and be resurrected. His love and His patience are vast, but He is not a doormat. One day He will declare, "Enough is enough."

Think & Talk

How have you taken God for granted?

Consciously look for ways to recognize God's hand in your day-to-day life. Help your children know how blessed they are to have a God who loves them, wants to know them, and be known by them.

Fun Times with Younger Kids

Needed: 2 kinds of dried pasta, bowl, large spoon

Let your child add one large spoon of dried pasta to the bowl.

Say: Let's say that this pasta is the right things God wants us to do.

Now, add a spoon of the other dried pasta to the bowl.

Say: Let's say that this pasta is the wrong things that God does not want us to do. We need to get these sorted out. We don't want the wrong things mixed in with our right way to live.

Preschoolers love to sort, and it's so good for them! Everyone should participate in this sorting exercise. Each time a piece of the first pasta is removed from the bowl, the person will tell something that pleases God. Put it back in its container. Each time a piece of the second pasta is removed from the bowl, the person will tell something we can do or say that would not please God. Put it back in its container.

Fun Times with Older Kids

Needed: 2 kinds of dried pasta, bowl

Put a handful of one kind of dried pasta in the bowl.

Say: This represents the wrong beliefs the people of Assyria had. They believed in gods that didn't exist.

Now, add a handful of another kind of dried pasta to the bowl.

Say: This pasta represents true beliefs in the One True God.

Mix the two pastas together.

Say: As the years passed and all the beliefs were mixed together, the people couldn't remember what was really true and what was false. Right and wrong had gotten all mixed up! What can you do if you don't know if something is really what God desires? If you have questions, you can go to the Bible. If the Bible says that it's not true, then you know it's not true. The Bible is one way God helps us know exactly what He wants. Can we take the pastas apart? Sure, we can! It's tedious and takes time to sort through them, but we can. When you search and take your time, God will help you understand what is true and what He does not approve of.

THE BIBLE IS OUR GUIDEBOOK FOR LIVING.

Josiah and the Forgotten Book
[2 CHRONICLES 34–35]

Egermeier's **Bible Story Time**

Read "Josiah and the Forgotten Book" in your *Egermeier's®
Bible Story Book.*

Story Background

READ PSALM
119:11.
WHAT ARE
SOME WAYS
YOU CAN
HIDE GOD'S
WORD IN
YOUR HEART?

Most of the time the leadership of Judah was weak or wicked, but a few times good men found their way to the throne. Josiah was one of the good guys. He renovated the temple and got rid of the idols that other kings had allowed to be erected there. One of the workers found a book while cleaning out one of the temple rooms. When the priests and scribes examined it, they found it to be the Book of the Law written by Moses. This document was the reason the temple and the worship that was conducted there existed. The fact that it had been lost is a testimony to how far the Jews had fallen from what God expected. How could God's people hope to be who He wanted them to be and to do what He commanded them without knowing the Law He had given Moses? Josiah led the people to a great spiritual revival that grew out of simply reading the Word of God and making the choice to follow its commands.

Someone once said that if all the Bibles today were picked up off the shelves and dusted off in homes all over the world, it would cause the biggest dust storm the planet has ever known. In many parts of the world, the Bible languishes in bookcases or closets. Even though it contains words that change lives for the better, brings peace to people and between people, and creates hope for this life and the next, it is ignored. People are desperate for help with their problems and to find purpose for their lives, and often the very answers they seek are already in their possession. Wisdom, hope, love, salvation, and peace are at their fingertips.

Are you taking advantage of the words God gave us? Or are those words collecting dust and lost for your family?

Think & Talk

Here's a simple plan:

Take the challenge to discover what God's Word for your life is by reading the Bible. A few minutes each day adds up. (Five minutes each day will add up to 152 hours of reading in just one year!)

Find a translation that is easy for you to understand.

Ask God to help you apply what you read to your life situation.

Open your heart and life to God's Word to you.

Determine to think and act the way God commands.

IS YOUR FAMILY READY FOR THE READ-THE-BIBLE-IN-A-YEAR CHALLENGE?

Fun Times with Younger Kids

Needed: old paper/newspaper, kitchen tongs, Bible, garbage bag

Say: When the temple was being cleaned of all the rubble, the high priest found a scroll with God's words written on it. This was a wonderful find! How exciting! Josiah wanted to hear every word of what was written there. He also wanted the people to hear it and obey it.

Fill the garbage bag with paper wads made from newspaper or scraps of used paper. Lay the Bible on the floor and dump all the paper wads on top of it. The object of this game is to pick up a paper wad with the tongs and put it back in the garbage bag until you find the Bible. (If you just have one set of kitchen tongs, then take turns.) Keep removing the paper wads until none are left on top of the Bible; then pick it up. The person who removes the last paper wad from on top of the Bible will say, "I found the God book!"

Fun Times with Older Kids

Needed: pick up sticks

Say: Every time we read the Bible or hear someone talk about it, God reminds us who He is and what He is like. Each time we open it, it's like uncovering a treasure. The Bible teaches us how God wants us to live and encourages us to be faithful to follow Him.

Play a game of pick up sticks as a family…with a twist. Each time a stick is successfully removed, the person picking up the stick will tell something he/she has learned from the Bible. If he mentions a person's name (like "I learned about Jonah"), then he should tell what he learned about God by finding out about that person.

HOW IS THE
BIBLE LIKE
BURIED
TREASURE?

Jeremiah in the Dungeon
[JEREMIAH 37–52]

Bible Story Time *Egermeier's*

Read "Jeremiah in the Dungeon" in your *Egermeier's® Bible Story Book*.

Story Background

When he was a young man, Jeremiah was called by God to be a prophet. God warned Jeremiah that even though he would share God's words, the people would not listen. That is not exactly the career path a young man would choose to hear from the Lord. Nevertheless, Jeremiah spent his life speaking up for God. Some people think that prophets are people who see into the future; however, the primary function of a prophet is to speak the words God gives him. Sometimes these words refer to the future or to outcomes in the future, but most prophecy has to do with attitudes and actions. The words God gave Jeremiah to say were often unpopular and rubbed important people the wrong way, but Jeremiah spoke with courage. He was thrown into a grimy dungeon and later into a cistern so mucky his friends had to pull him out with a rope. Still, Jeremiah said what needed to be said, and as God told him, few people listened.

A CISTERN IS A DEEP, ROCK-LINED HOLE IN THE GROUND USED FOR COLLECTING RAINWATER.

Jeremiah came near the end of a long line of great prophets who warned Judah that God would not always put up with their idol worship and flaunting of His laws. Because they had escaped the Assyrians by a special miracle, the people of Judah thought they would not suffer the fate that had befallen the kingdom of Israel. They were half right. Assyria didn't conquer Judah and destroy Jerusalem, but Babylonia, an even greater empire from Mesopotamia (the area now known as Iraq), did. The Babylonians took almost all the Jews captive to serve in their great cities, and they utterly destroyed the temple and the walls of Jerusalem. Jeremiah was permitted to stay in Jerusalem where he wept and wrote the books of the Bible we know as Jeremiah and Lamentations.

GOD DOES NOT
PROMISE US
EASY LIVES;
HE PROMISES
TO BE WITH US.

Just because God asks you to do something doesn't mean that it will be easy. Some people think if life is hard, they must not be doing God's will. The truth is that God does not promise any of us easy lives. Instead, He promises to be with us. God needs dads and moms, as well as boys and girls, who will persevere when times are difficult and speak up for Him when it is unpopular.

Think & Talk

Name a particular situation where you need wisdom to know when to take a stand for God in your family, at school, at work, and/or in the community.

Having courage isn't easy. Sometimes it seems almost automatic and other times, it's difficult to find. When is it most difficult for you to have courage? When do you have to put up with opposition and ridicule?

When do your kids see you taking a stand? Is it for something important or merely to get your way?

Fun Times with Younger Kids

Say: Jeremiah warned the people that God was not happy with the way they kept worshiping idols and gods that weren't real. What does a warning do? It gives you a signal that you'd better watch out or something bad might happen. What does a smoke detector do? When it beeps, it's telling you the house is getting full of dangerous smoke. When the gas light comes on in the car, what is that warning you of? It's telling you it's time to go to the gas station. When the timer goes off for the cake that's baking, what should you do? Take the cake out of the oven before it burns! What other warnings do you know about?

As you drive around town, point out warnings you see to remind your child that Jeremiah warned the people to obey God, and these signs/signals/alarms warn people of possible danger in the community.

Needed: red-skinned apple, mini-marshmallows, alphabet cereal/pasta/pretzels

Slice 2 wedges of the red-skinned apple for each person. Put them together on a plate so that the raw edges are touching to resemble lips. Then use some mini-marshmallows to make teeth.

Say: God told Jeremiah to warn the people, but he was very young, and the people didn't want to listen to him. Even so, Jeremiah kept saying what God wanted him to say. The words God told him to say kept coming out of his mouth.

Use the alphabet cereal, pasta, or pretzels to write out a warning.

Daniel in the King's Court
[DANIEL 1]

Egermeier's Bible Story Time

Read "Daniel in the King's Court" in your *Egermeier's® Bible Story Book*.

Story Background

Nebuchadnezzar, the Babylonian king who took the Jews captive, had great power, great wealth, and *some* wisdom. Instead of reducing all the Jews to manual slave labor, he had them placed in jobs for which they were suited. Some took administrative positions. Of course, this caused jealousy among Babylonians who thought they should get those jobs—a circumstance that set the stage for some of the drama that took place among the Jews during the captivity.

Daniel, along with his friends, Hananiah, Mishael, and Azariah (better known by their Babylonian names Shadrach, Meshach, and Abednego) were among the Jews who were specially trained to work for the king. At the end of their three-year training course, they had a meeting with Nebuchadnezzar. By the time they met the king, the young men had not only learned the language, but also the wisdom of Babylon. The king found them to be the wisest of his men, and they were given very good positions.

From these young Jews we can learn to make the best of our circumstances. Daniel and his companions could have rebelled, played dumb, or become flatterers. Instead, they stood their ground on some important things, like Jewish dietary restrictions, yet were willing to learn many other things from their captors/instructors. Perhaps they had learned from the story of Joseph how they should act when captive in a foreign land. Daniel and the others excelled and were put in positions of trust, which allowed them to have influence with the king to the advantage of their people.

LIKE JOSEPH, DANIEL HAD THE GOD-GIVEN ABILITY TO INTERPRET DREAMS.

Think & Talk

Are you in a spot that is less than ideal for a Christian? Do people around you misunderstand or even ridicule your faith? How can you become an asset to your group or company without compromising your walk with Christ?

What vibes do you send to the people around you? Are you known as a competent, caring individual, or as a judgmental curmudgeon?

What can you do to best reflect Christ at work, at school, or in your organization? Do you need a change of attitude?

Fun Times with Younger Kids

Needed: socks, 2 buckets

On one bucket write "GOOD." On the other write "BAD." Roll a few pairs of socks into themselves to make soft balls. Place the buckets next to each other against a wall. Take turns tossing the socks. If a sock ball goes in the "GOOD" bucket, then the tosser must name one food that is good for you to eat. If a sock ball goes in the "BAD" bucket, then the tosser must name one food that is not nutritious (even if it's yummy).

Say: Daniel and his friends wanted to eat the nutritious food they were used to eating, instead of eating the king's food. They proved to the king that they would be healthier and better servants if they could eat their nutritious food.

TAKE A PEEK IN THE PANTRY. HOW MANY HEALTHY FOODS CAN YOU COUNT? HOW MANY UNHEALTHY?

Fun Times with Older Kids

Say: Daniel and his friends were conscious of what they ate because, in the first books of the Bible, God lays out guidelines for a healthy diet. In those days, there wasn't a government agency that checked to make sure food was safe, and there weren't many safe ways to store food, like in refrigerators or cans. What did Daniel and his friends eat? They ate vegetables and drank water. Are those good for you today?

Teaching your kids to make good choices when it comes to food is very important. Use Daniel and his friends as inspiration to keep you and your kids on track.

Download a great, free app called Fooducate. As you walk through the grocery store, your kids can scan the barcodes of different packaged foods. The app will give the food a grade (just like in school) and tell you the sugar content. It's a quick, fun way to evaluate each food right there in the store and make smart choices, instead of waiting until you have it at the house and then trying to avoid it.

The Fiery Furnace
(DANIEL 3)

Bible Story Time *Egermeier's*

Read "The Fiery Furnace" in your *Egermeier's® Bible Story Book.*

Story Background

Jews in Babylon walked a fine line between faith in God and compromise with the king. It was particularly difficult for those in powerful positions like Daniel's three friends: Shadrach, Meshach, and Abednego. When the ego of Nebuchadnezzar went into overdrive and he ordered a 90-foot-tall golden statue of himself built so people could worship him, the three friends had to take a stand…literally. When the music sounded and thousands bowed to the 9-story-high statue, Shadrach, Meshach, and Abednego stood up and stood out like telephone poles on a prairie landscape. Their courage was immense because the penalty for not bowing to the statue was immediate execution by fire.

TO SEE WHAT HAPPENED TO NEBUCHADNEZZAR, READ DANIEL 4:28-37.

Nebuchadnezzar's advisors were thrilled that the three Jewish men put themselves in this position because they had been hoping for a way to get rid of these foreign interlopers who had found favor with the king. The king had declared that anyone who didn't bow would burn in the furnace, but he didn't want to give up three of his best men. King Nebuchadnezzar called the three to himself to offer them a second chance. The answer of Shadrach, Meshach, and Abednego is a classic statement of deep faith, "Our God can deliver us from your fiery furnace, but even if He does not, we will not worship any idol." They believed that God could find a way to keep them out of the fire if He chose to do so. God could have done something to quench the fire, or he could have struck down the king, but their faith went beyond some quick, simple solution like that. They would remain faithful, whatever the outcome, because they trusted God completely.

God chose to bless them in a way they could not have imagined. They were thrown into the frightfully hot furnace, but they were not burned, and when the king peered into the furnace he saw a fourth person with them who looked "like the Son of God." In other words, God met them in the furnace. In the moment of most extreme calamity, in the moment of total hopelessness, God was present to save them. Sometimes the worst thing that could happen, the thing we dread most, the thing we pray won't happen, happens. Deep faith, like that of these three young men, trusts God even then. In that moment of deepest despair, the Lord meets us and becomes more real to us than ever before. It takes simple trust that goes beyond trying to get things to go our way, and believes that God has a way for us that may be beyond our understanding.

Think & Talk

Do you have "even if he does not" faith? Or is your faith more an "I will trust You, God, if You make it easy for me" faith?

Do you trust God to love you and see you through even the most difficult circumstances? Think about a challenging time in your life. When in the timeline of that situation did you put your trust in God? Was it as a last resort when you didn't know what else to do? Or was it from the very beginning?

Ask God to deepen your faith. Ask Him to help you trust Him like Shadrach, Meshach, and Abednego did. If you are going through a furnace time right now, don't wait…ask God to meet you right now.

Fun Times with Younger Kids

Needed: 2 big baskets/tubs, rolls of toilet paper

Say: Can you say the names of the three men who were thrown into the fiery furnace? They were Shadrach, Meshach, and Abednego.

Encourage your children to say each name after you several times. It may be funny to listen to your preschoolers try to say these names, but they're anxious to repeat anything and everything after you.

Say: But when the king looked into the furnace, he saw four men walking around. He said the other one looked like the Son of God.

Set 2 large baskets or tubs against a wall. Gather all the rolls of toilet paper in the house. Two players will stand about 6-feet from the baskets with the supply of toilet paper. At the signal, the two players will bend over, facing away from the baskets, and begin hiking toilet paper rolls at their basket with the goal of getting four in. Each time a roll goes in, they will shout one of the names: Shadrach, Meshach, Abednego, Son of God!

Fun Times with Older Kids

Needed: spool of thread

Say: Do you think you can break this thread with your bare hands?

Let one of your kids try, and he/she should be able to. Now, ask your child to hold his/her hands out with wrists together. Wrap the thread around and around them 15-20 times.

Say: Now, try to break the thread. Your faith is like this thread. When you wrap it around your life, when it's part of everything you do and say, and when you exercise/use your faith, then difficult times won't destroy it. Shadrach, Meshach, and Abednego were closely bound to the Lord. They had relied on God all their lives, so when the threat from King Nebuchadnezzar came and they were thrown in the furnace, their faith was not destroyed. They didn't back down when there was pressure from the outside.

IF YOU EXERCISE YOUR FAITH, IT WILL BE STRONG ENOUGH FOR ANY CHALLENGE.

Daniel in the Lions' Den
[DANIEL 6]

Read "Daniel in the Lions' Den" in your *Egermeier's®* Bible *Story Book*.

Story Background

DANIEL WAS OVER 80 YEARS OLD WHEN HE WAS THROWN IN THE LIONS' DEN.

Like his three friends, Daniel had to stand his ground in opposition to a command of the king. In his case, the king was Darius, and the issue was prayer. By this time the Persian Empire had conquered Babylon. Jealous Persian officials fed Darius' ego and convinced him he should declare that for one month all requests should be made to him and not to any god, real or otherwise. They knew that Daniel would not obey this law, so they had it worded in such a way that even the king himself could not repeal it. They had discovered Daniel's habit was to kneel every day by his window facing Jerusalem and pray to God. Of course, he was caught.

The prescribed fate for violators of the law was to be thrown to lions. Darius had a high opinion of Daniel and the depth of his faith, but the sentence had to be carried out. When Daniel survived the night in the lions' den, Darius was the first to rejoice. He even threw the men who suggested the law into the den. (One wonders why he didn't think of that before.) Then he wrote letters to all corners of the empire, telling about Daniel being saved by God from the lions and with the recommendation that everyone worship Daniel's God.

Daniel got into trouble for simply doing what he always did to stay close to his Lord. His enemies tried to ruin him because of it, but God turned their plot into a way to make his name known throughout the empire in the highest level of society. God uses people when they are faithful. Ironically, Daniel did many great things, both for God and in his job for Babylon and Persia, but the thing that brought him the most recognition then and now was his simple habit of prayer.

We must not forget to do the little things that strengthen our relationship with the Lord. With a busy schedule filled with urgent matters, it's easy to put aside important things that don't call as loudly for our attention. Daniel knew it was urgent to refrain from praying for a month, but he also knew it was important for him to pray. Prayer turned out to be far more important than he ever could have imagined.

Think & Talk

How are you doing with your routine spiritual disciplines (prayer, Bible study, worship, service, witness, giving)? Are you practicing them or are you putting them off? Spiritual disciplines are exercise for your soul—they're holy habits. You can put them off, but as with physical exercise, you will find yourself weaker and less healthy if you do. Ask God to help you to exercise holy habits.

THE BIBLE HAS MUCH TO SAY ABOUT PRAYER.

How are you teaching these holy habits to your children? Now is the time to lay that groundwork!

Fun Times with Younger Kids

Say: Three times a day, Daniel got down on his knees and prayed at his window. What do you see when you look out your window?

Little ones are learning about prayer, and it's important to keep them from getting into a rut in how they pray. In the Bible, we see people praying in all different ways, many times very physically, in different places, for different reasons. This is a great opportunity to show variety in your prayer time by encouraging your child to kneel alongside you at the window and pray like Daniel did. You don't want to do this all the time because that would just create a new rut, but this week try praying like Daniel.

READ
2 CHRONICLES 7:14,
JAMES 5:13-16 AND
1 THESSALONIANS 5:17.

Fun Times with Older Kids

Needed: play dough

Kids and grown-ups love to play with play dough! Get the play dough out and use it to create the entire scene of Daniel in the lions' den. The jaws of the lions were locked shut by God, so they couldn't harm Daniel. With that in mind, while you are working on your play dough, talk to one another...but with your lips closed firmly together. No one can open his/her mouth!

When the project is completed, you can open your mouth to really understand one another. Talk about the courage that Daniel showed.

Say: Under what circumstances do you need extra special courage?

Queen Esther Is Troubled
[ESTHER 4:4-17]

Bible Story Time

Read "Queen Esther Is Troubled" in your *Egermeier's® Bible Story Book.*

Story Background

Esther was a real-life queen whose story rivals the best fairytale princess stories. This young Jewish girl, living in exile, won a kind of beauty contest to become the wife of King Ahasuerus. No one, not even the king, was aware of her ethnicity. When one of the king's social-climbing advisors made being Jewish a crime punishable by death, Esther's uncle Mordecai sent a message, asking her to intervene for her people. Of course, Esther was saddened by the news of the plot, but she was struck with fear for three reasons. First, the king didn't know she was a Jew, and she didn't know if he would be angry because she had not told him. Secondly, asking for an audience with the kind was a breach of protocol. The normal procedure was to wait until the king sent for her. And lastly, because she was a Jew, she was under the same death sentence as all the rest.

Mordecai urged her to speak up in spite of her fear. He told her that perhaps God had enabled her to become queen for this very reason: "for such a time as this." She took courage, approached the king, and saved the Jews.

The courage this little beauty queen demonstrated was significant, especially in light of the fact that the former queen had been dismissed for a breach of protocol. She could have chosen to protect her secret, but she came forward to save many.

Sometime it will be your turn to stand up for what's right. Sometime you will have to take a risk to do the right thing. Don't let fear keep you from doing the very thing God placed you in your situation to do. This may mean not going along with something shady at work or in your social circle. It could

QUEEN VASHTI LOST HER CROWN FOR REFUSING TO COME SHOW OFF HER BEAUTY AT THE KING'S PARTY.

also mean having courage to steer your children away from situations that tempt them, which you know to be dangerous—a stand that may not make you popular with your kids. Taking a stand holds the risk of being unpopular and worse, but perhaps you are the one chosen to speak the truth or do the right thing at this moment in time.

Think & Talk

When have you been troubled about whether or not you should take a stand or speak up? Are you struggling with that situation now? What are your options?

STAND UP FOR JESUS!

Share with your children when you have taken a stand and how you did that in a godly way. This is an incredibly important way to encourage them and give them strength to do likewise when their time comes.

Pray for God's wisdom to know when to speak up, what to say, and how to say it.

Fun Times with Younger Kids

Needed: dress-up items, camera

Take turns dressing a member of the family as a king or queen—that means you too, parents. The kids will enjoy "decorating" you! Get out pieces of material and old jewelry. You can use a towel paper roll, giftwrap roll (cut down), or a kitchen utensil for a scepter. If you don't have a play crown, then make one by stapling two pieces of construction paper together. Take a photo of each person when his/her costume is complete.

Fun Times with Older Kids

Needed: a book

Say: Esther spent a year preparing to be the queen. She practiced her posture and was trained to walk like a queen. Queens are very stately and carry themselves gracefully. Esther also had obstacles that made her choices difficult. What were some of those obstacles? If she went to the king without him asking her to come, she could be killed. She wasn't sure how the king would react to her being a Jew. Esther had a big request to make of the king.

Place some pillows or obstacles throughout the room and indicate a path around them. Then each person will pretend to be Esther, balancing a book on his/her head while walking the path. Good posture, everyone! Walk like royalty!

The Walls of Jerusalem Are Rebuilt

[NEHEMIAH 2:19–6:19]

Read "The Walls of Jerusalem Are Rebuilt" in your *Egermeier's® Bible Story Book*.

Story Background

Gradually, the Persian policy toward the Jews changed, and they were allowed to move back to Judah. By the time Nehemiah became a servant for King Artaxerxes, the temple in Jerusalem had been rebuilt and some Jews were living in the city; however, the walls still lay in ruin. Without walls, a city in those days was always in danger from any neighboring community or roving bands of robbers. Jerusalem would not be a safe place until there was a protective wall around it with gates that could be secured.

Nehemiah received permission and backing from Artaxerxes to leave his service and lead the rebuilding of the wall of Jerusalem. It was an ambitious project because the city was only partially repopulated. Some of the citizens ridiculed the job as being too big. Neighboring towns protested—the last thing they wanted was a strong Jerusalem. They knew if the wall was completed the city would repopulate.

Nehemiah put all the people in Jerusalem to work. Because of the outside threat, they had to go to work armed. Amazingly, they finished the walls and hung the gates in 52 days. Fifty-two days…think of that. In less than two months, they made Jerusalem a functional city and a safe place for the return of the Jews still in exile.

God gave Nehemiah a dream—a new wall for His city—and Nehemiah let nothing deter him from this task. He had to get the king to release him from his job and grant permission for the project. Next, he had to convince the people in Jerusalem it

KING XERXES IN THE ESTHER STORY WAS THE FATHER OF KING ARTAXERXES. VASHTI WAS HIS MOTHER.

could be done. Then he had to deal with threats from outsiders. Finally, there was the challenge of actually doing the task. This is a great lesson for us: when we are convinced that a dream comes from God and is not just our own wishful thinking, we must pursue that dream with the persistence of Nehemiah.

Think & Talk

What dream do you have? A college degree for yourself or for your children? A good career? Or perhaps your upbringing was not a good experience for you and your dream is to make your family a great launching pad for your kids.

Ask God to plant His dream in your heart. Ask Him to help you pursue His dream for you no matter what obstacles come your way. Ask Him to let you see His dream come true for your life.

PURSUE GOD-GIVEN DREAMS WITH PERSISTENCE!

Fun Times with Younger Kids

Needed: lots of disposable cups

Say: Nehemiah led the people to build the wall around the city of Jerusalem. The wall protected the people from their enemies, so it was very important.

Your little ones will love learning how to build a cup wall. Start off with a base of 5 cups. Show them how to place 4 cups on the next layer so that each cup straddles two cups under it. Once they master this, then start with more cups on the base. This is a great exercise for their fine motor skills and brain development. For added fun, show your kids a YouTube video on speed stacking or cup stacking. Speed stacking uses special plastic cups, and part of the exercise is to bring down the wall as well as build it.

Fun Times with Older Kids

Needed: regular and mini-marshmallows, regular uncooked spaghetti (not angel hair), table covering

Cover a surface with placemats or a plastic tablecloth because this project could get a bit sticky.

Say: You probably have some kind of official building blocks that we could build a wall out of, but let's try doing it out of a surprising resource—marshmallows and spaghetti.

Together, create a wall as stable as you can make it, using both regular and mini-marshmallows. Snap pieces of spaghetti the length you need to run between the marshmallows in order to keep them from sliding.

Say: What materials do you think Nehemiah and the workers used for the wall around Jerusalem? (Google "wall around Jerusalem" to see lots of photos of what this story is about.)

Bonus Activity:

When you're done, melt the marshmallows with margarine and add some rice cereal to make some crispy treats. Create a new wall with crispy treat bricks. Which is stronger? Why?